ERI[
A TOUR[

...R.E.A.

...st Guide

Robert Papstein

The Red Sea Press, Inc.
Publishers & Distributors of Third World Books
11-D Princess Road
Lawrenceville, New Jersey 08648

THE RED SEA PRESS, INC.
11- D Princess Road
Lawrenceville, New Jersey 08648

Copyright © Robert Papstein, 1995

Photographs: Robert Papstein
Book Design: Linda Nickens

Library of Congress Cataloging-in-Publication Data

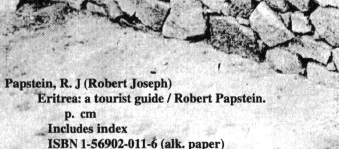

Papstein, R. J (Robert Joseph)
      Eritrea: a tourist guide / Robert Papstein.
           p. cm
      Includes index
      ISBN 1-56902-011-6 (alk. paper)
      1. Eritrea--Guide books. I.Title
DT393.P37 1995
916.3504'72--dc20   95-10362
                                                           CIP

REA

*To world travelers
everywhere.*
R.P.

TABLE of

8	*Basic Facts About Eritrea*
	(Quick Reference to Important
	Addresses and Telephone Numbers
	P. 11)
12	*Foreword*
13	*Introduction*
22	Cautions
23	Before You Go
23	Tourist Information
23	Health
24	Best Times to Visit Eritrea
25	Planning a Budget: Money & Prices
26	Languages
26	Social Customs
28	Arriving and Departing
28	Visas
28	Travel to Eritrea
28	Air
30	Overland
31	By Sea
31	Departing from Eritrea
34	What to Bring
34	Clothes
34	Personal Supplies-Medicines
35	Books of Interest About Eritrea
37	Religions / Nationalities
38	Travel Within Eritrea /Asmara
38	Rail
38	Buses
38	Taxis
41	Renting a car
41	Driving yourself
41	*Driving documents*
42	*Road conditions*
43	Currency
43	Credit Cards
43	Tipping
44	Hours of Business
44	Public Holidays
45	Time
45	Weights-Measures-Distances
45	Sizes
46	Electricity
47	Photography
50	Crime and Theft
52	*ASMARA*
52	*Basic Facts*
56	Tourist Information & Services
56	Communications Post Office
57	Phone System
57	Fax Services
57	Express-Courier Services
58	Banking
58	Goverment Offices
58	The University
59	Libraries
60	Newspapers & Magazines
60	Emergencies: Medical /Police
62	Accomodation-Hotels
62	Eritrean Food
67	Water
68	Restaurants
71	Buying Food
74	What to See
74	National Museum
75	The Markets
76	Places of Worship
78	Tsetserat / tank graveyard
78	Cinemas and Opera House
79	Coffee and Cafés
80	Lunches-Snack Bars
81	Shopping-Gifts
81	Leather
81	Shoes
82	Gold-Silversmiths
82	Handicrafts
83	Nightlife
83	Arts
83	Sports
84	*One Day Trips from Asmara*
84	Keren
84	Serejeka--Zager--Sabur--Murar
85	Mendefera
86	*Multi Day Trips from Asmara*
86	Massawa
86	Axum
89	*MASSAWA*
89	*Basic Facts*
92	Travel to Massawa
92	Debre Bizen Monastery
93	Getting Around Massawa
93	What to See
94	Where to Stay
96	Resturants
98	Visiting the Dahlak Islands
98	Scuba Diving
98	Sport Fishing
99	Hunting
100	*ORGANIZATION OF GOVERNMENT*
101	Government Offices
	Addresses and Telephone
	Numbers
103	Eritrean Embassies Abroad
104	Bilateral Agencies
105	International NGOs
106	Local NGOs
106	Multilateral Agencies
107	United Nations Agencies
108	Foreign Representations, Embassies
	and Consulates
110	*MAP*
	Africa and where Eritrea is
	located plus provincial map of
	Eritrea.
112	*INDEX*
118	*CITY MAP OF ASMARA*

6

CONTENTS

ERIT

BASIC FACTS ABOUT ERITREA

Size: 124,320 sq. km (47,754 sq. miles) About the size of England, Austria or the American State of Pennsylvania.
Neighboring Countries: Ethiopia, Sudan, Djibouti. Saudi Arabia and Yemen across the Red Sea.

Capital: Asmara (population 400,000)

Population: 3.5 million

Ethnic Composition: 9 nationalities

Principal Working Languages: Tigrinya, Arabic, English. English is the most commonly used western foreign language and is the medium of instruction in secondary schools and university.

Flag: Green, red and blue with a gold olive wreath.

Emblem: Camel

Major Urban Areas: Asmara (capital), Massawa, Assab.
Ports: Massawa, Assab on the Red Sea
Currency: Currently using Ethiopian birr but plans to eventually issue its own currency.
Two tiered rate of exchange: Tourist rate   USA $1 = @ 6.20 birr,
                                                                    Eritrean rate USA $1 = @ 7.20 birr.
GDP per Capita: US $75-150
Infant Mortality Rate: 135 per 1,000 births.
Life Expectancy: 46 years
Adult Literacy Rate: 20%
Population per Doctor: 48,000
Population per Nurse: 1,750

Form of Government: President and National Assembly. Following the UN Supervised Referendum in April 1993 in which 99.8% of the population chose independence. The Provisional Government of Eritrea became the Government of the State of Eritrea with a four year mandate to draft a democratic constitution which guarantees the rights of all citizens, creates political pluralism and establishes an elected government.

Economy: In 1994 Eritrea was in a process of transition. During the Ethiopian occupation virtually all resources were nationalized by the government and in most cases compensation paid to the former owners. The Eritrean Government inherited this state of affairs in 1991 and since that time has sought to privatize state owned enterprises. Some complain this process is proceeding too slowly; others counter that this is necessary to ensure that Eritreans have the opportunity to become the owners of their own economy. Government encourages foreign investment.

Commercially Exploitable Mineral Reserves: iron, copper, gold, potash and potentially oil and natural gas.

Commercially Exploitable Agricultural Resources: During the Italian colonial period (1890-1941) Eritrea produced agricultural products for export, particularly cotton. The country's potential for commercial agriculture is presently under study. Eritrea has significant potential for commercial fishing from the Red Sea.

ERITREA

QUICK REFERENCE TO IMPORTANT ADDRESSES/NUMBERS

For medical or police assistance ask your hotel to contact the appropriate authorities on your behalf if necessary.

Airlines
Eritrean Airlines: 12-5501,12-5500, Fax: 11-4775 Harnet Avenue
Lufthansa: 12-5501, 12-5500, Fax: 11-4775 Harnet Avenue
Egypt Air: 12-5501, 12-5500, Fax: 11-4775 Harnet Avenue
Ethiopian Airlines: 12-7512, 12-6827 Harnet Avenue No. 89-91
Saudia Airlines: 12-0166, 12-0156 Harnet Avenue
Sudan Airways: 12-0604 Harnet Avenue No. 37
Yemeni Airlines: 12-5501, 12-5500, Fax: 11-4775 Harnet Avenue

Hotels
Asmara
Ambassador Hotel: 12-6544, Fax: 11-6545
Ambasoira Hotel: 12-3222, Fax: 12-2595
Hamasien Hotel: 12-3411, 12-3657
Keren Hotel: 12-0740
Nyala Hotel: 12-3111, Fax: 12-2914
Selam Hotel: 12-7244, Fax: 12-0662

Massawa
Dhalak Hotel: 552725
Red Sea Hotel: 552710
Gourgusum Beach: 552522

Keren
Keren Hotel: 14

Assab
Zerai Deres Hotel: 660245

A full list of government offices and their telephone numbers appears on page 101.

FOREWORD

If you are looking for international mass tourism, Eritrea is not the place for you. But if you are looking to visit a new country in which people are happy to see you, willing to share their culture and lives, there is no place in Africa quite like Eritrea. It is a travelers place, rather than a tourist destination. What you will find is a new, dynamic country, friendliness and extremely good value for money. This is the time to go if you are interested in seeing this part of the Horn of Africa.

Tourism will inevitably grow in Eritrea, but for the moment most visitors are government officials, representatives of international organizations, Eritreans returning for visits after many years in exile, journalists, film makers, and those wise enough to know that here is a fascinating part of Africa which offers incredible cultural and geographical diversity.

This guide is intended to provide the basic information that visitors need. It has especially taken into account the needs of business visitors to Eritrea.

Coverage is concentrated on the capital, Asmara, and the major tourist destination of Massawa. In the future we hope to expand the guide to cover other regions of Eritrea more comprehensively. Because Eritrea is changing so rapidly it is inevitable that information will go out of date and new information will need to be included. We would like to hear about your experiences in Eritrea and will make every effort to include relevant new information or corrections in future editions of *Eritrea: A Tourist Guide.*

Please write to us at The Red Sea Press, Inc., 11 Princess Road, Suite D, Lawrenceville, New Jersey, USA, 08648. Fax 609-844-0198.

INTRODUCTION

On May 24, 1993 Eritrea celebrated its first Independence Day: it is Africa's newest state. Eritrea is located in northeastern Africa facing the Red Sea. It is bordered by Sudan to the west and north, and by Ethiopia and Djibouti to the south. It has an area of 125,000 sq. km. (over 48,000 sq. miles), comparable to the size of England, Austria or the American State of Pennsylvania. It has an estimated population of 3.5 million but it will take a proper census, something which has never been carried out in Eritrea, to know more precise figures.

Ethnically Eritrea is divided into nine nationalities. These are (in alphabetical order) the: Afars, Bilen, Hedareb, Kunama, Nara, Rashaida, Saho, Tigre and Tigrinya. About 70% are agro-pastoralists, 20% traders-workers, 9% pastoralists and 1% fishermen. Geographically, Eritrea includes a central highland region, the Danikil desert in the southeast, and lowland regions located on either side of the highlands.

Although Eritrea has a number of urban centers, the capital Asmara and the ports of Massawa and Assab are the most important. The majority of the population lives in rural areas. Approximately a quarter of the population is at least partially nomadic, making this one of the largest remaining nomadic populations in Africa and the world.

Administratively, Eritrea is currently divided into the following provinces each with a capital city or town (see map). In the near future these provinces will be redrawn.

Akele Guzai--Adi Qayeh	Asmara City---Asmara
Barka--Akordat	Dankalia--Assab
Gash & Setit--Barentu	Hamasien--Asmara
Sahel--Nacfa	Semhar--Massawa

Eritrea is unique. Although it was once an Italian colony, it has had a very different historical experience from virtually all other African countries. Its newly won independence was no the result of European colonial powers relinquishing authority rather it is the result of thirty years of war in which virtually the entire Eritrean nation sacrificed and struggled. It is hard to imagine that there is a single Eritrean family which did no lose a son or a daughter, a wife, husband, father or mother in the struggle, and many Eritrean families lost much more. In order to understand contemporary Eritrean attitudes, the things you will see and the context in which you will see them it is necessary to understand Eritrea's background and recent history.

Maps of Africa from the late nineteenth century show the Italian colony of Eritrea alongside the myriad of other colonies of Africa. On maps of Africa made in the mid-1960s, where the ex-colonies are now represented by their newly independent names, Eritrea has disappeared as an independent political entity. The most recent maps of Africa

Before it became an Italian colony at the end of the 19th century, Eritrea had a rich and varied history reaching back to the 3rd century B.C. when outposts of Ptolemaic Egypt were established in the region. During the rise of the Axumite Kingdom, a precursor to modern Ethiopia, much of the region of modern Eritrea was in Axum's sphere of influence; between the 1st and the 9th centuries, the port of Adulis and later Massawa became transhipment centers for the trade of the Red Sea into the interior of the Horn of Africa. The connections to Axum were of special importance because Axum was a center of Orthodox Christianity and its commercial and religious influence spread widely in the region.

Various parts of Eritrea were, at times, controlled by the several Beja kingdoms between the 13-16th centuries, the Fun sultanates of Sennar in the Sudan, the Abyssinian kingdom between the 14-18th centuries and again at the end of the 19th century when the Kings of Shoa began to unite the region into what eventually became modern Ethiopia. In the 18th century Egypt under Muhammad Ali was influential in areas of Eritrea and between the 16th and 19th centuries the Ottoman Turks were the dominant power, especially along the coast.

Eritrean societies reflect this richness and diversity of historical contacts, perhaps most vividly in their adherence to the ancient Orthodox form of Christianity and in their early acceptance of Islam which spread across the Red Sea from the holy cities of Mecca and Medina in Arabia.

The modern boundaries of Eritrea are largely the product of European competition for African colonies and especially Italian colonialism. Italy began to occupy areas along the Red Sea coast in the late 1860s and eventually declared the creation of the colony of Eritrea on January 1, 1890.

The Italian colonial period began gradually but ended abruptly in 1941 with Italy's defeat in the Second World War. Of Italy's colonies (which included Libya and Italian Somaliland), Eritrea was regarded as the jewel in the crown. Not only did Italy intend to use Eritrea as a base for its wider imperial ambitions in the Horn of Africa, particularly against Ethiopia (which fascist Italy conquered between 1935-1941), but its Mediterranean climate in the highlands, its agricultural potential and rapidly developing small scale industrial infrastructure led to what was expected to be the permanent home of 50,000 Italian settlers.

When the Fascists came to power in Italy, Eritrea's strategic position became even more important. Italy had been disastrously defeated on the plains near the town of Adua in 1896 when it attempted to conquer Ethiopia. Mussolini was determined to avenge this humiliation, which stuck in the throat of Fascist *machismo,* and to conquer Ethiopia which had hitherto escaped European colonialism. The Italians also knew that the outbreak of war in Europe would mean the immediate closure of the British-controlled Suez canal to Italian shipping. As a result, Mussolini's government embarked on an aggressive program of industrialization and infrastructure improvement in Eritrea so that the colony would be capable of supplying the Italian army in Africa. By the end of the 1930s Eritrea was one of the most highly industrialized colonies in Africa albeit on a small scale. It was exporting fruit and other agricultural products to Italy, had small scale industries capable of supplying local needs as well as export markets and boasted a railroad, system of roads and tele-communications unique in the region.

With the Italian defeat in 1941, Great Britain, which was the major European power in the area through its control over Egypt, the Sudan and parts of Arabia, established a military administration over Eritrea while the United Nations debated the future of the Italian colonies. British rule lasted for a decade, until 1952. Eventually, Libya and Italian Somaliland were granted independence but Eritrea, against the wishes of the majority of Eritreans, was denied self-determination and was federated to Ethiopia for strategic reasons.

The Emperor of Ethiopia, Haile Selassie, who in a dramatic speech before the League of Nations, had shamed the western world for its failure to do anything against Italian aggression in the mid-1930s,

was reinstalled on his throne in 1941. He returned American support for Ethiopia's regional imperial ambitions, principally the Eritrean Federation, by granting the United States a major military base in Asmara, the Eritrean capital. Kagnew Base (now called Denden) was the most important communications and radar control center for the region. It was staffed, over the years, by thousands of American troops and brought an overlay of American culture and attitudes and an emphasis on the English language to Eritrea.

The unpopular Federation of Eritrea with Ethiopia went into effect in 1952 but was unilaterally abrogated ten years later when in 1962 Haile Selassie dissolved the Eritrean parliament and annexed Eritrea as Ethiopia's fourteenth province. Despite Eritrean protests the United Nations did nothing. Eritrea simply disappeared into Ethiopia, and from the maps of Africa.

In 1961, when it was clear that Ethiopia had no intention of honoring its commitments to the Federation and that the United Nations and the United States would not oppose Eritrea's annexation, a few frustrated reformers turned revolutionaries attacked a police station, stole some pistols and began a struggle for Eritrean independence which would last more than 30 years, cost 65,000 Eritreans their lives, drive a third of the population into exile to live as refugees or displaced persons and launch Eritrea on a policy of self-reliant development unique in Africa.

In 1964 the Organization of African Unity convened for the first time: its president was Emperor Haile Selassie. It met in the Ethiopian capital Addis Ababa, which became its permanent home. The first order of business for the OAU and its new member states was the problem of what to do with Africa's colonial-created borders. Even though it was widely acknowledged that colonial borders which divided peoples arbitrarily between two or even three national states had led to many injustices, it was also widely felt that if these borders were allowed to be challenged, it would create chaos in Africa. Thus, the OAU declared the borders of Africa as they existed in 1964 to be fixed and permanent. This was a catastrophe for Eritrea which was arguing that it had been illegally annexed by Ethiopia two years earlier and was seeking a peaceful solution to what was an unresolved colonial question. The OAU decision had the effect of abolishing Eritrea as a legal entity and rewarded Ethiopia's aggression. Since all OAU members were obliged to respect the decision and other world governments aligned their policies on Africa to OAU policy, Eritreans had no other recourse but to fight for their independence.

For a decade the Eritreans struggled against the army of Haile Selassie, arming themselves with weapons they captured in abundance, gradually converting their rag-tag guerilla force into what was described in the 1980s as "the best guerilla army in the world." By 1977 about 90% of Eritrea was in the hands of Eritrean fighters. This long process of struggle, of self-sacrifice, self-discipline, political isolation and international indifference, forged an attitude of self-reliance that is the ideological foundation upon which contemporary Eritrea is based.

In 1972 a ferocious famine gripped Ethiopia and Eritrea. Haile Selassie's government at first ignored the famine, assuming it was the occasional fate of the peasantry to starve. Then, when it became clear that there was enormous internal objection to such a callous policy, provided too little assistance, too late. In 1974 a revolt in Ethiopia overthrew Haile Selassie and brought a new Marxist, pro-Soviet military junta to power. Called the Dergue, it ran the country for 17 years and was led by Mengistu Haile Mariam.

The Soviet Union and its eastern European dependents, anxious to increase their influence in Africa, came to the military support of the Dergue, eventually supplying military advisors and billions of dollars of military aid. Ironically, the Soviet Union, which had originally supported Eritrean Independence during the original United Nations debates over Eritrea's future, when Ethiopia was an American sphere of influence, now threw all of its might into the attempt to crush the Eritrean Liberation Front and later the Eritrean People's Liberation Front (EPLF), which spearheaded the struggle for independence.

In 1978, facing new Soviet-supported large-scale warfare, which included Mig fighters and bombers against which they had no air defense, the EPLF made what it called a "strategic withdrawal" into what is now Sahel Province in the northeast of Eritrea. Today, many

Eritreans hold special regard for those who were "in Sahel."

In Orota, the impregnable base camp in Sahel, the Eritrean People's Liberation Front (EPLF) turned the seeming disadvantage of its political and economic isolation into its greatest strength, an iron-willed self-reliance. Eritreans both inside and outside of Eritrea began to create a military, organizational, industrial and political infrastructure which would eventually bring virtually all of Eritrea into the struggle against the Dergue and which would lead to their ultimate victory.

Between 1978-1986 the Dergue launched eight major offensives against the EPLF. Some of these offensives were of World War II scale with combined ground, air and naval support.

By the end of 1989, after the EPLF had broken out of the World War I like defensive trenches they had held for a decade and were marching on a crumbling Ethiopian Army, the Soviet Union warned the Mengistu Government to seek a political solution in Eritrea, a warning also sounded by Mengistu's allies in East Germany, Bulgaria and Rumania who were also under internal political pressure and could offer less and less assistance. Mengistu refused the warning and in February 1990 the EPLF captured the port city of Massawa, which was then heavily bombed by the Dergue, severely damaging one of the most unique towns on the Red Sea coast. In May of 1991 the EPLF took Asmara, the capital. Facing simultaneous defeats by other armed opposition movements within Ethiopia, President Mengistu fled the country abandoning his routed armies in the field. Ethiopian soldiers captured by the EPLF were disarmed and sent home in a remarkable gesture of reconciliation. The EPLF had always maintained that it was the Dergue and not the Ethiopian people which was the enemy, even though dreadful atrocities had been carried out against Eritrea.

In May 1991, the EPLF established the Provisional Government of Eritrea. Its first order of business was to ask the United Nations to acknowledge the responsibility that it had ignored for so long and to supervise a referendum in which Eritreans, on the basis of "one person one vote", would be asked whether they wished to become independent or to remain a part of Ethiopia. The referendum, the first free and fair election ever held in Eritrea, took place at the end of April 1993 with 99+% of the registered population voting. On April 27, 1993 the result of the referendum revealed that 99.8% of Eritreans had voted for independence.

On May 24, 1993 Eritrea formally reappeared on the African political map and celebrated its first independence day.

Eritrea was welded together by the experience, sacrifices and self-discipline required by what is called "The Struggle". Its attitudes, official and unofficial were created by "The Struggle". Its political philosophy, its sensitivity to the plight of others, its sometimes seeming stubbornness in the belief in its own way of doing things---all of this comes directly out of the knowledge that only through self-reliance would they survive from one day to the next--which they did for a generation.

20

REA

The Eritrean population that lived as refugees or displaced persons scattered in Africa, the Middle East, Europe, North America and elsewhere donated a regular part of their incomes to sustain The Struggle. For those who remained inside Eritrea, everything was deferred or subordinated to The Struggle; families, careers, education---any semblance of a normal life. For a generation Eritreans lived under occupation or as fighters "in the field" (the term used to describe liberated Eritrea)---under punishing conditions which tested even the most committed.

This is the personal experience of virtually everyone you will meet in Eritrea. It is the key to understanding the country.

CAUTIONS

About Prices

Eritrea is changing quickly--virtually everything is being improved after years of neglect during the Ethiopian occupation. Prices are inevitably going to increase but in order to give an idea of the very inexpensive prices in Eritrea the US dollar has been converted at $1 = @ 6.2 birr.

About Street Names

Most street names have remained the same since Independence, with some important exceptions. The main street, once called Haile Selassie Avenue is now called Harnet Avenue (Freedom Avenue). At the top of Harnet Avenue, the road which leads in the direction of the airport is now called Martyrs Avenue, recalling the 65,000 Fighters who gave their lives in the struggle. Some other major street names have been changed and it is expected that more changes will come in the future.

Important Information About Telephone Numbers

Because the telephone system in Asmara and elsewhere in Eritrea was badly neglected in past decades, it is currently undergoing major renovation and modernization; this will mean changes in telephone numbers, and in some cases new area codes. The country code for Eritrea is now 291 and the code for Asmara is 1. Asmara uses the prefixes 11, 12, 16 and 18 and then the telephone number. To call Asmara from outside of Eritrea, dial your international access code plus 291-1 and then the number.

Important Information About Dates

In addition to the Roman calendar of 12 months used in the west, Eritrea also uses the Julian, also called the Ge'ez or Coptic, calendar for certain events. This calendar divides the year into 12 months of 30 days and one month of 5 or 6 days, and is one week behind the Roman calendar. The Roman calendar is used for all official occasions and government documents but for Christian religious events the Ge'ez calender is used. This means that Easter in Eritrea (which follows the Julian calendar) is later than in western countries that follow the Roman calendar; in 1993 it was one week later and in 1994 it was three weeks later. In calculating years the Ge'ez calendar is 7 years behind the Roman calendar. 1965 in the Ge'ez calendar is 1972 in the Roman.

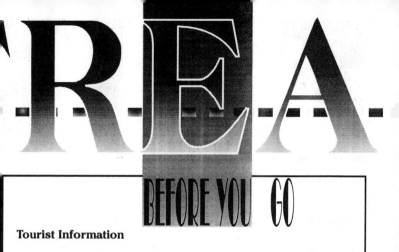

Tourist Information

USA and Canada
The best source of information about Eritrea in North America is the Embassy of Eritrea to the U.S. located in Washington, D.C. Tel: (202) 429-1991 and the Consulate of Eritrea to Canada, located in Ottawa Tel: (613) 234-3989. Should a separate Tourism Office be created, they can direct you to it.

Great Britain
Government of Eritrea, Mission to the United Kingdom, 96 White Lion Street, London N1 9PF. Tel: 071-7130096. A List of Eritrean Embassies in other countries appears on page 103. They can either provide information or direct you to an Eritrean Tourist Office.

Health
Eritrea has a very healthy climate, especially in the Highland areas. Some would say that Asmara has an ideal climate, very similar to the Mediterranean or California. However, the lowlands, especially along the coast, can be hot and humid, particularly in the summer months of June-September. Although malaria is not more widespread in Eritrea than in other parts of Africa, it is essential to take an anti-malaria preventive if you are travelling to malarial areas, principally the lowland and coastal regions. As Asmara itself is at 2,350 meters (7,000 feet), malaria is virtually non-existent and most residents of the capital, including foreigners, do not take anti-malaria preventatives. Malaria has proven extremely resistant to many of the earlier malaria drugs and new, more effective preventatives are now available. Your doctor will be able to recommend the best one for you.

It is best to carry an International Vaccination Card in which all of your inoculations are listed. Once you have finished the series of injections and the card is completed it is wise make a photocopy of the card and put it in a safe place. Some of the

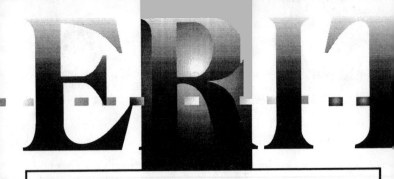

injections are effective for ten years and it is senseless to have them again if the card is lost.

For Eritrea (as for virtually all parts parts of Africa and Asia) the following inoculations are necessary:

1. Yellow Fever
2. Cholera
3. Typhus
4. Tetanus

Other inoculations are often recommended such as Polio and Hepatitis A.

It all sounds rather daunting, but two visits to your physician will do it and some are now oral rather than injected inoculations.

Visitors to Eritrea should also take a good sun protection cream, especially if traveling in the lowland regions. A hat is also important and for those with particularly sun sensitive skin, a total sun blocker cream is wise insurance.

Do not assume that you can buy any prescription drugs locally--take sufficient quantities with you. While Eritrea has an excellent pharmaceutical manufacturing facility, they only produce a limited range of drugs.

Best Times To Visit Eritrea
For the Highlands including Asmara:
Virtually anytime, but December and January can be cold. The hottest time is April-June.

For the Lowlands including the coastal areas:
December-February, where the average temperature is in the mid-20's Celsius (70-80 Fahrenheit).

During the hottest months, June-August, coastal temperatures can reach into the 40's Celsius (90+ Fahrenheit).
Rains start in May-June and last until September.
Greenest time: June-July-September-October

MONEY & PRICES

Prices
Eritrea must be regarded as one of the best-value-for-money destinations in Africa. Prices are very low. An adequate hotel room can be found for US $10 or less; a first class room for $45.00; an Italian dinner with local wine or beer at $5.00; cappuccino is 15 cents.

Types of Currency
At the time of writing, Eritrea continues to use the Ethiopian birr (100 cents to one birr). The rate of exchange is US $1 = @ 6.20 birr. Sometimes people quote you prices in "dollars" but they really mean birr---check before paying. This is not an attempt to cheat you but rather a hold-over from the days of a large American military presence in Asmara.

What Types of Currency to Bring
The preferred type of currency is the US dollar. Other currencies can be exchanged at the larger banks but for convenience the US dollar is by far the best.

Exchange Rates
The best exchange rates are at the banks; the hotels offer slightly less.

Travelers Checks
Eritrea has had virtually no tourism for the past twenty years but businesses are adapting rapidly to current travel practices. Travelers checks are increasingly used in Eritrea but they are virtually unknown outside of Asmara, Assab and Massawa. When traveling outside of Asmara it is best to carry sufficient cash. Travelers checks can be cashed at the major Asmara hotels and at the banks.

Credit Cards
For better or worse, credit cards are hardly used in Eritrea, even in Asmara. While credit cards may become common in the future, be prepared to pay in cash or with travelers checks.

Languages

Eritrea has 9 different nationalities, each speaking its own language, but English is the defacto working western language. In addition to the local language Tigrinya, Arabic is also widely spoken, especially along the coast. Many older people speak Italian.

Social Customs

Eritreans are extremely polite and courteous. Unlike the people at many tourist destinations, Eritreans are actually happy to see you and will go out of their way in cafés and elsewhere to see to it that you have a place or come to your help if there is confusion in ordering.

Eritreans are also proud; they paid a terrible price for their independence and they are secure in the knowledge that they did this themselves, with little support outside their own community.

are no beggars, and even though they have an up-hill struggle to restore the city to its former beauty, the fountains work and the public clocks run on time.

Don't be surprised if someone greets you on the street or asks you how you like Eritrea and where you come from. These are not street hustlers: 99 times out of 100 they are genuine expressions of interest and pleasure that you have come. Take the initiative; a simple greeting will inevitably be reciprocated. Very few tourists have visited Eritrea in the last twenty years. Until 1991 most Eritrean contacts with Westerners were with Soviet or East Block military advisors. People are sometimes hesitant at first, but once initial hesitations are overcome you will be treated as a guest in a country with a great tradition of hospitality.

ARRIVING &

Visas and Entry information into Eritrea

All visitors to Eritrea require a visa. This is easily obtained from the Eritrean embassies listed on page 103. To obtain your visa, you need to send your passport or travel document valid for at least six months from your date of visa application and one recent passport-size photo. This is applicable at the time of writing. Necessary forms, applicable fee rates and up-to-date information can be obtained from the Eritrean embassies. Service is usually prompt and efficient, but it is sensible to allow sufficient time for processing and return mail. For a small extra fee passports will be returned via express or registered mail. If time is short they might be willing to fax you the visa forms.

Travel to Eritrea

By Air

Airlines

Asmara International Airport, Tel: 18-1822.

Eritrean Airlines is now just beginning domestic service and promises to be one of the best operated airlines in the region. 89 Harnet Avenue, P.O. Box 222, Asmara, Tel: 12-5501, 12-5500, Fax: 11-4775.

Egypt Air, P.O. Box 222, Asmara, Tel: 12-5501, 12- 5500, Fax: 11-4775.

Ethiopian Airlines, P.O. Box 5245, Asmara, Tel: 12-7512, 12-6827. Harnet Avenue 113. Ethiopian Airways has, at present, the most flights to Eritrea. Most of them via Addis Ababa but, some also arrive directly from Europe (London and Frankfurt) stopping first in Asmara and then continuing on to Addis Ababa.

Visitors flying to Asmara on Ethiopian Airlines must reconfirm their return flights as soon as possible after arrival. The office is often full and unless you are there early expect a wait. Ethiopian Airlines no longer accepts currencies other than birr so it is necessary to first change money before buying the ticket. Some passengers have been asked to show their bank conversion receipt prior to issuing the ticket.

Travelers in-transit in Addis Abeba should be aware of the following:

*A Transit Visa can be obtained at the airport for a fee of 10 birr. You will be required to leave your passport at the airport and given a pink temporary

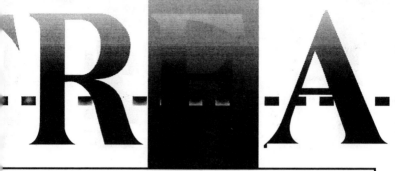

DEPARTING

visa card, which is also the receipt for the passport. Upon departure, after checking in, you will receive your passport back at the immigration control point in the airport. If you have stayed in Ethiopia less than 24 hours you do not have to pay the US $10 departure tax. Ask for a blue exemption ticket.

✴Ethiopian Airlines has a policy of paying for a forced overnight stay (when there is no connection) only when the incoming fare is 700 birr or more. In practice this policy means that visitors heading in the direction of Asmara will be accommodated, even for the day, but, because the Asmara-Addis flight is slightly less than 700 birr Ethiopian will not provide overnight accommodation for travellers flying Asmara-Addis Ababa even if they are continuing on Ethiopian Airlines the following day. Regardless of what your travel agent (or Ethiopian Airlines) tell you, this rather unfortunate policy is enforced at the airport in Addis Ababa. This may not be currently applicable.

✴Even transit passengers are required to fill in a currency declaration. You will receive a receipt for money changed at a hotel. Any excess birr you may rechange into dollars at the airport---with the original exchange receipt.

✴A peculiarity of the Addis Ababa Airport is that you must have a baggage handler carry your bags across the street from the airport buildings to the taxi stands or to those waiting to collect you. Normally this costs 2 birr.

✴The older (blue) taxis charge about 15 birr to take passengers into the center of Addis Ababa. The newer taxis have meters and higher rates.

✴Addis Ababa has a wide variety of hotels from the luxurious and expensive Hilton to the simplest pension. The Ghion, Ethiopia and Wabi Shebelle are tourist class hotels. If you are looking for atmosphere try the Taitu Hotel in the old part of Addis Ababa. This was the first hotel built in Addis Ababa and it is built in a grand style with large rooms overlooking the city. A first class room (with toilet and bath) is US $37 per night. The hotel is old and showing its age but still has an ambiance hard to find in modern hotels. The reception staff is very helpful.

Out the door and to the right and around the corner on the major street is a small restaurant serving Italian and Ethiopian food--good and inexpensive. One of Addis Ababa's best (and expensive) Italian restaurants is just nearby; ask at the reception for directions.

ARRIVING & *DEPARTING continued*

Lufthansa, 89 Harnet Avenue, P.O. Box 222, Tel: 12-5501, 12-5500, Fax: 11-4775. Offers twice weekly flights from Frankfurt to Asmara with a stop in Cairo. Lufthansa may expand its service to Asmara, check with them for current schedules.

Saudia Air, P.O. Box 95, Asmara, Tel: 12-0166, 12- 0156. On Harnet Avenue. Flys to Asmara via Jeddah.

Sudan Airways, Harnet Avenue 37, tel: 12-0604 also flys to Asmara via Khartoum. This once-proud airline has seen a serious decline in service in the past years and has not always been helpful to international passengers in transit in Khartoum.

Yemenia Airways, P.O. Box 222 Asmara, Tel: 12-55- 01, 12-5500, Fax: 11-4775. Flys to Asmara from Sanaa.

By Land

From Sudan
For the very adventurous there are Sudanese buses-trucks which are traveling into Eritrea from the Sudanese town of Kassala and possibly from Gedaref. However, the political situation in Sudan is in a state of flux and Sudanese-Eritrean relations have been strained by border

incidents; and Western travelers are experiencing increasing difficulty with Sudanese officials.

From Ethiopia
Overland travel is relatively easy from Addis Ababa with a 4 wheel drive vehicle. Main Eritrean roads, mostly built during the Italian colonial period, are asphalted but suffered neglect and war damage during recent years. The Ministry of Construction and the Eritrean Army are engaged in a crash program of road repair and improvement. Eritrea has a surprisingly good road system between the major towns. The roads in the direction of Ethiopia are especially good. They were improved by the Mussolini government far beyond their local utility in order to facilitate the Italian invasion of Ethiopia in 1936.

By Sea

For travelers arriving from the Gulf region, boat services between the Gulf and Eritrea will certainly increase and this may be an inexpensive alternative to air travel in the future. Freighters and small local boats do make the trip regularly. It is increasingly difficult to travel with freighters these days and the trip by local boat includes its own risks. It's possible, but it can also take a long time to arrange and to travel; not something to consider if you have a fixed period of time. The only ports with customs and immigration clearance at present are Massawa and Assab.

Departing from Eritrea
Departing non-Eritrean visitors must pay a US $10 departure tax at the airport plus a security check tax of 3 birr.

Check with your airline as to how long in advance prior to the flight you are required at the airport. Usually they ask you to be at the airport at least 2 hours prior to departure. It is essential to reconfirm your flight reservations, especially with Ethiopian Airlines.

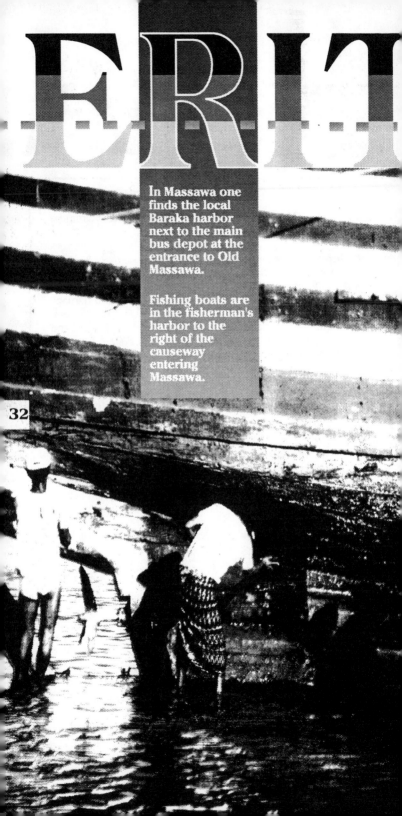

ERIT

In Massawa one finds the local Baraka harbor next to the main bus depot at the entrance to Old Massawa.

Fishing boats are in the fisherman's harbor to the right of the causeway entering Massawa.

33

WHAT TO BRING

Clothing: What to Wear

Whatever you decide to wear, 100% natural fabric is best. The highland areas of Eritrea have an ideal, Mediterranean type of climate but the lowlands can be hot and the coastal areas hot and humid.

While traveling around Eritrea can be sometimes adventurous, it does not require special "safari" clothing. The Kenya game park industry has sold this image to visitors---and not a small amount of clothing as well--but loose fitting, natural fibre clothes are sufficient. If your itinerary requires a good deal of walking, a comfortable pair of walking shoes is not a bad idea. Safari "boots" are good, as are training shoes.

Generally speaking, informal dress is the rule in Eritrea. However, many men prefer a jacket and tie and women, especially in the evening, dress very fashionably.

In November-February the highland areas, including Asmara, can be cool even during the day and refreshingly chilly in the evenings. A sweater and light coat are advised. Given the opportunity, Eritreans are stylish dressers in both traditional and western clothing. You will not see women (or men) in shorts, tank tops or other highly revealing clothes. This is offensive to both Muslims and Christians who have a clear idea of acceptable dress which does not include, even at the beach, mini-bikinis or topless. You will definitely have a more enjoyable stay if you fit in.

Personal Supplies

Medicines/Prescription Drugs

Most basic non-prescription medicines are available in Asmara, although the brand selection might not be large. Pharmacies are scattered throughout the city and are relatively well stocked. Anyone requiring special prescription medicines would be well advised to bring sufficient supplies and a prescription for the medicines which indicates the generic, rather than brand name. In the event of loss the medicines might be available locally under the generic name. Women visitors to Eritrea will find sanitary towels available but again, the selection could be limited, and it would be prudent to bring a sufficient supply.

Cosmetics are available and while the selection is limited the range of all goods in the shops is growing rapidly.

BOOKS OF INTEREST ABOUT ERITREA

The Africa World Press and its sister press The Red Sea are the major publishers of books about Eritrea. The list below reflects some of the contemporary writing about Eritrea of interest to visitors, some of it by Eritrean authors. The books cited reflect some of the most recent publications in English and those which are likely to give the reader the best insight into the experiences of Eritreans.

Novels
Thomas Keneally, *To Asmara*. A novel of the Eritrean struggle by the former Booker Prize winner.

Bereket Habte Selassie, *Riding The Whirlwind*, 1993. *An Ethiopian and Eritrean story of love and revolution.*

History/The Struggle for Independence
Abeba Tesfagiorgis, *A Painful Season and a Stubborn Hope: The Journey of an Eritrean Mother,* 1992. Autobiography.

Dan Connell, *Against All Odds: A Chronicle of the Eritrean Revolution,* 1993.

Robert Papstein, *Eritrea: Revolution at Dusk,* 1991. A photojournalistic and oral history of the last years of the Eritrean struggle for independence.

Roy Pateman, *Eritrea: Even the Stones are Burning,* 1990. Perhaps the best and most readable introduction to Eritrean history and politics.

Local professional organizations publish regular reports concerning their activities. See for example the publications of the National Union of Eritrean Women, Eritrean Medical Association, and Eritrean Relief and Rehabilitation Agency. In addition, there is now a weekly English language government newspaper, *Eritrea Profile.*

ERIT

RELIGIONS AND NATIONALITIES

Religions

Eritreans are approximately half Christian, primarily Orthodox with small numbers of Catholic and Protestants and half are Muslims, mostly Sunnis and some Sufis. A small percentage of the population hold other traditional African religious beliefs.

Nationalities

Eritrea comprises nine nationalities and, as Eritreans jokingly say, a tenth---those who have lived as refugees outside of Eritrea for many years. The nationalities of Eritrea and their languages are:

```
Afar-------Afar
Bilen------Bilen
Hedareb----To Bedawi
Kunama-----Kunama
Nara-------Nara
Rashaida---Arabic
Saho-------Saho
Tigre------Tigre
Tigrinya---Tigrinya.
```

While most people today participate in a variety of economic activities, in a general way the lifestyle of Eritrean nationalities can be divided as follows:

80% Rural, of which 70% are agro-pastoralists,

    9% Pastoralists (Nomads)

    1% Fishermen and

20% Traders-workers

TRAVEL WITHIN ERITREA

Rail

The Italian-built railroad from the port of Massawa to Asmara, Keren and Akordat was one of the early casualties of the war. It is now being rebuilt. In its heyday it was a genuine feat of railroad engineering ascending gradually from sea level up the base of the steep escarpment and then up the escarpment face into Asmara, a rise of some 2,400 meters. It then continued down to Keren and Akordat in the western lowlands.

Bus

Buses and mini buses are the mainstay of the urban and especially the rural public transportation system. Eritreans have a long tradition of technical excellence and although many of the buses are old they are in good repair. New buses are now increasingly seen and the government's commitment to safe, cheap, efficient public transportation is an indicator that this sector will improve considerably in the next years. Travelers who want to see the countryside and who do not have access to an automobile have few alternatives but to take the buses. For long distance buses between towns operators are required to limit ticket sales to the number of available seats.

Buses depart Asmara from a variety of locations. One of the principal points of departure is at the fuel station next to the Cathedral but there are other bus depots around the city.

Taxis

Eritrean taxis are the ultimate testimony to Eritrean mechanical skills. Many of the older taxis are of indeterminate age and probably have few, if any, original parts left in them. They come in all sizes and shapes, many of them very personal statements of interior decoration by their drivers. Until recently they were painted blue but

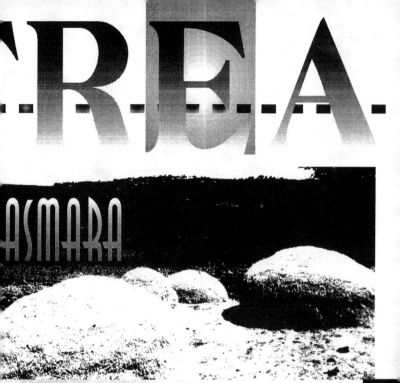

most have now been repainted yellow in imitation of the new taxis. None have meters and you must make out a price with the drivers, but they are inexpensive. Virtually any destination within Asmara can be reached for 5-15 birr.

If you have been terrified by wild, high speed taxi rides in other parts of the world, Eritrea will come as a great relief. Limited fuel supplies, the fragility of the old taxis and common sense combine to result in a leisurely trip. At times everything seems to be moving in slow motion, but one always arrives safely and relaxed.

In addition to the fleet of old taxis, new "yellow" taxis are being introduced. These do have meters but they are not always used. The government encourages private ownership and entrepreneurship and therefore the new taxis are intended to be exclusively owner-driver.

Taxi Routes

Some taxis cruise regular routes--the main thoroughfares and major destinations. If you hail a taxi along one of these routes it will stop even if it already has passengers. You may travel along this route getting out at any point for 1 birr (20 USA cents). If you ask the taxi to deviate from the main route, even a small deviation, the taxi will ask for 5 birr (or more) anywhere in central Asmara (if they have no meter) or the price on the meter if a yellow taxi.   See also mini buses next page.

Contract Taxis

These are taxis which do not run on fixed routes. You will see contract taxi stands here and there around Asmara. They will take you where ever you wish; best to fix the price before departure.

From Airport to Asmara

A taxi costs about 45 Birr plus 5-10 Birr for luggage. The price seems to keep going up but there is an official price and taxis are not allowed to charge more. If you are charged what seems to be a high price, write down the number of the taxi and complain to the Tourist Office.

"Businessmen's Taxi"

If you have many visits to make in a morning it can be wise to hire a taxi for 3 or 4 hours. The taxi will wait for you at each stop. Expect to pay between 50-60 Birr for this service.

Mini Buses

There are small buses following fixed routes and stop when hailed; price is 1 birr. They are small government owned and operated buses, stopping for passengers and letting passengers out as they follow their route. These often go to popular destinations such as hospitals or outlying residential areas.   In response to the competition from the mini buses taxis are now offering a similar service.

RENTING A CAR

Driving Yourself

The Eritrean Tour Service (Harnet Avenue #61 Tel: 12- 4929) offers self drive automobiles. The newly renovated hotels are also preparing to offer chauffeur driven or self-drive automobiles. A chauffeur driven car is not much more expensive than a self drive and certainly worth investigating. The drivers are good; they know the city and often serve as informal guides pointing out places of business and tourist interest.

Some prices from ETS to use as a guide:

Per day:	In City	Out of City	Km price	Free km. inside city	Free Min km. outside city
Toyota Corolla	150	300	2.50	40	50
Land Cruiser	350	450	3.00	40	75
Minibus 5-14	450	850	3.50	40	75

All rental cars require a refundable deposit of 1,000 birr.
Eritrean Tour Service is the largest rental agency. It also operates through the major hotels.   Another firm is Amico Rent A Car, Tel: 111551, St. Francisco St. Kaliev #33, Asmara.

Drivers are available for 50 birr per day plus 10 birr per hour after 8 hours.

Driving Documents

In order to rent a car you must be at least 25 years old and hold either a valid Eritrean or International Driving License. At present, long term visitors working in Eritrea must submit their drivers license and obtain a temporary Eritrean license.

Maps

Maps are available in Asmara from bookshops and from the Tourist Office--when they have them. The Michelin road maps of Africa are very useful and widely available in Europe and the United States. The most widely available map in Eritrea is out of date for the Dankalia Province: the coastal road between Massawa and Assab is hardly useable and the military road which passes through the interior is not indicated. Anyone seeking to make this trip or to visit the Dankalia Depression should contact Eritrean Tour Service, whose drivers are experienced in this very remote area. The Ministry of Tourism has prepared new Tourist maps of Eritrea and Asmara. These are available from the Tourism Department, Eritrean Tour Services and bookshops.

Road Conditions

The improvement of infrastructure is one of Eritrea's priorities. The Ministry of Construction is following a crash program of road improvements. The quality of Eritrean roads has improved greatly in the past few years. Certainly the roads between the major towns are safe and relatively comfortable. Prudent drivers will be especially cautious at night when domestic animals can stray onto the roads.

CURRENCY

Eritrea continues to use the Ethiopian birr as its official currency. The dollar is the preferred currency for exchange. Arriving visitors will find a bank at the airport offering competitive rates of exchange, although it is rather slow when many people are waiting.

Importing Currency into Eritrea
There is no limit on the amount of currency one is entitled to import.

Black Market
Black market currency dealing is limited in Eritrea but will be punished, even for tourist offenders. This is definitely something to avoid.

Grey Market
Merchants will sometimes offer to accept dollars in lieu of birr. They "exchange" at the tourist official rate (6.2 birr to the dollar) and then exchange at the bank using the higher Eritrean resident rate. A merchant does not have authority to accept dollars.

Importing other valuable articles
You are entitled to import items such as personal computers, cameras and video cameras for your own use but you are not entitled to sell them. If you have a personal computer or video camera, you will be asked to register the serial numbers at the airport upon arrival.

Rates of Exchange
Tourist rates are likely to fluctuate but only slightly--at the time of writing the rate was 6.2 birr to one US dollar. Some of the luxury hotels offer slightly less. Eritreans are allowed to exchange at the higher rate of 7.2 birr.

The vast majority of visitors to Eritrea accept that the tourist exchange rate is a legitimate means of the Government to raise much needed revenues to face the staggering costs of national reconstruction.

Tipping
In most hotels and their restaurants a 10% service charge is included in the price. Some people leave a small tip. In cafés there is often a dish for tips.

HOURS OF BUSINESS

Government Offices
Government offices open at 8:00. They close again at 12:00 and open at 14:00 to 17:00.

Shops
This varies, with most shops opening between 8-9 and closing again until 2 or 4 and then opening until 8.

Public Holidays
Eritrea follows the Roman calendar (12 months) but for some events the Julian calendar is used. This means that some religious events calculated in the Julian calendar are one week later than in the Roman calendar. In addition, Muslim holidays follow a lunar calendar and therefore their dates change each year.

National Holidays
New Year's--January 1
Women's Day--March 8
Labor Day--May 1
Independence Day--May 24
Martyr's Day------June 20
Start of the Armed Struggle--September 1
Christmas--December 25

Religious Holidays
Timket (Epiphany)--Variable (January)
Eid el-Fitr--variable (Spring)
Fasika (Easter)--variable (April)
Eid el-Adha--variable (Summer)
Eid al-Nabi (Prophets birthday--variable, Summer)
Meskel--variable (September 27)
Lidet (Christmas)--(Julian or Ge'ez calendar, January 7)

TIME

Eritrea uses the 24 hours clock, sometimes called the Military clock. 0:00-12:00 hours is 12:00 midnight to 12:00 noon. The system differs from the AM-PM system only after 12:00 noon. 12:00-24:00 hours is 12:00 noon to 12:00 midnight. Therefore 13:00 hours is 1:00PM; 14:00 hours is 2:00PM; 24:00 hours is 12:00 PM. Once used to it, the system prevents any confusion between AM and PM and is the reason why all airlines, the military and an increasing number of countries use the 24 hour clock.

Eritrea time is GMT (Greenwich Mean Time) plus 3 hours. There is a two hour time difference (ahead) between continental Europe and Eritrea, except when Europe is on Summer time; then the difference is only one hour (ahead).

There is an eight hour time difference (ahead) between USA Eastern Standard Time and Eritrea, which is reduced to seven during Daylight Savings Time.

There is a one hour time difference (ahead) between Eritrea and the Sudan.

WEIGHTS, MEASURES, DISTANCES

Eritrea uses the metric system. Foodstuffs are sold accordingly: 100 grams, 200 grams etc., 500 grams is roughly equivalent to an American-English pound and 1,000 grams is a kilogram or 2.2 pounds.

Distances are calculated in meters and kilometres. 2 centimeters is nearly one inch. One meter is approximately 3 feet; one kilometer 0.6 miles.

Sizes
Although the metric system is the standard size of measurement for clothing, the only truly effective way of getting a proper fit is to try it on. Assistance in shops is helpful and friendly.

ELECTRICITY

The Italians used 110-120 volts as their standard voltage. Ironically when the Americans, who normally use 110 volts came in the 1950s they standardized on 220 volts. Eritrea uses both voltages at present. Most houses are also equipped with 110 and 220 volts. Both voltages run at 50 herz, which is slower than the US standard of 60 hertz. Hotels tend to have 110-220 sockets. Usually there are two sockets in the wall: the one with the inserting pins farther apart is the 220 socket; the one with the narrower pins is 110. During the war this system was not always used and the only sure way to know is to test. Adapters are available in most electrical shops.

When considering the use of electrical appliances in Eritrea purchased abroad, both the voltage and hertz (formerly cycles) can be important. Too much voltage (220 volts used on a 110 appliance) will ruin it and the wrong hertz will affect the performance of the appliance especially those such as cd players and record and cassette players which must run at a certain speed. Make certain that both the volts and hertz are compatible. It is possible to adapt the voltage but usually not the hertz requirements of an appliance. Many appliances are capable of operating on both 50 and 60 hz--this is usually indicated on the appliance. Laptop/notebook computers usually use a power supply which automatically adjusts for voltage and hertz.

IMPORTANT

The flow of current on the 110 line in particular is highly variable. Equipment that is especially sensitive to power fluctuations should be used with a surge protector. Equipment intended for long term use in Eritrea should be protected with a stabilizer (available locally). Computer users should know that power supply cut-offs occur for anywhere from a few minutes to an hour or more. Computers should be backed-up frequently and connected to an emergency battery supply if possible.

Electrical supplies are widely available and those coming for longer stays can find the appropriate adapter plugs in electrical shops. The standard plug in the newer hotels is the Europlug--the standard two round prong plug now used in Europe. USA visitors will require a plug adapter available at electronics stores or locally in Asmara.

During The Struggle the Photography Section of the Information Department made extensive and effective use of still photography and video to communicate to exiled Eritreans how their donated money was being used for development projects as well as the state of the military situation. Their archive, which is meticulously catalogued, contains some 250,000 negatives and 5,000 slides.

Photography is permitted virtually everywhere in Eritrea. Visitors who have found paranoia about photography elsewhere in Africa will find Eritrea a welcome change. Obviously, discretion and a sensitivity to the privacy of others is required, but few formal photographic prohibitions exist. Normally, photography is not permitted at military installations. If in doubt, ask. It is, however, important to note that based on their religious traditions many Muslims, especially Muslim women, find photography objectionable and common courtesy requires photographers to exercise caution and to ask for permission prior to making photographs.

A photographic permit is not required. The National Museum charges a 50 birr fee for using video cameras. Still cameras are admitted free.

Asmara has a number of shops selling photographic supplies. In the past thirty years, during the Ethiopian occupation, little opportunity for photography existed but today photography is booming in Eritrea. Photographic shops are scattered throughout the city but there is a particular concentration in the area between the Government offices and the Cathedral.

Film/Developing
Fresh slide film (Fujichrome) is available in Asmara only, but there is no local developing. ISO 100 film is adequate for most situations. Some people who wish to photograph inside without flash will want to bring some ISO 400 film. Serious photographers taking slides will need to bring sufficient film with them. The film of choice for Eritreans is print film. Local mini-labs located in the photographic shops do excellent quality developing and printing in one hour or less. A roll of 36 exposure print film costs about 25 birr and processing and printing about 100 birr.

Heat damages film. The prudent traveler in Eritrea's warmer regions will try to protect film against excessive heat. Keeping film out of the direct sun and out of hot car glove compartments should be enough.

Special Equipment/Techniques
No special photographic equipment is needed in Eritrea. However a UV (ultra violet) filter over the lens to compensate for the extra UV at higher altitudes and to physically protect the front lens element against bumps is a useful addition. A rotating polarizer filter will give you stunning blue skies when used correctly. Take a set of extra batteries for your camera. Carry a lens brush, small plastic bottle of lens cleaning fluid, and a packet of lens cleaning tissues.

If you are going to be traveling in very dusty rural areas, a large plastic bag is the cheapest protection against the most common cause of camera failure, dirt. A large plastic trash bag can be used to protect the entire camera bag in very dusty conditions.

Much photography in Eritrea is done under conditions of extreme contrast: dark brown faces in bright sunlight often wearing white clothing. Often the exposure meter is fooled into giving too little exposure (due to the brightness of the sun and white clothes), resulting in underexposed and unrecognizable faces. Knowing this, the photographer can compensate by giving more exposure, but then the whites are "burned out" by overexposure. There are two solutions. The first is to reduce the contrast by making photographs in shady areas where the difference between skin tone and clothing is reduced. The second is to use a technique called fill-flash in which the primary exposure setting is determined by the camera as normal (which would result in underexposed faces) but the built-in (or accessory) flash "fills-in" the darker areas. When fill-flash is used correctly it can hardly be seen. Many modern cameras have this feature; the more expensive cameras have quite sophisticated fill-flash systems.

Video cameras are very popular and video cassettes are widely available. You will be asked to register the number of your video camera at the airport upon entry to ensure that you do not sell it while in Eritrea.

CRIME AND THEFT

Prudent travelers will not tempt fate; but Eritrea in general and Asmara in particular is a paradise for travelers accustomed to violent crime and theft in major tourist destinations world wide. Crime against tourists is virtually unknown.

No one handed Eritreans their independence, and they are rightly proud that they had achieved this through years of hard work and self-discipline. The Government tries very hard to provide basic services to the poor and unfortunate. During the years of the Struggle the EPLF set in motion programs to care for orphans, street children, women forced into prostitution through poverty and the physically and mentally handicapped. After independence these programs have been enlarged and are seen as a major responsibility of government. Eritreans do not look kindly upon beggars and there are very few on the streets--far fewer than in most western capital cities. Once when walking down the main street of Asmara two young boys asked me for money and when I declined they continued along with me repeating their requests with increasing urgency and insistence. Two Fighters (as soldiers are called) were walking behind me; they grabbed the boys by the scruff of the neck, lifted them up like limp rags and spoke to them quite directly. I didn't understand what they said but when I passed the same place a few days later the boys were there again and greeted me but definitely did not ask for money.

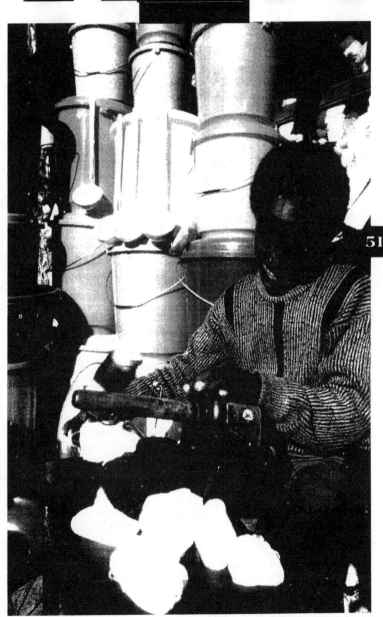

51

BASIC FACTS

Capital of Eritrea
Population: 400,000
Altitude: 2,350 meters
Climate: Pleasantly warm days and comfortable, cool nights
Hottest month: May
Coldest month: January

Although it would be easy to think of Asmara, the Eritrean capital, solely as an Italian built colonial city, its origins actually reach back some 700 years. Originally, it is said, there were four clans living in the Asmara area: the Geza Gurtom, the Geza Shelele, the Geza Serenser and Geza Asmae. Encouraged by their women, the men united the four clans and defeated the bandits who preyed on the area. After the victory, a new name was given to the place, *Arbaete Asmara* which literally means, in the Tigrinya language, "the four are united." Eventually *arbaete* was dropped and it has been called Asmara, though there is still a zone called *Arbaete Asmara*.

When the Italians conquered Asmara in 1890 they made it the capital of their new colony. The city was divided into two quarters: one for the Italians and one for the Eritreans. The exclusively Italian areas, called the Camp Estato, located on the hilly parts of the town, were rapidly developed.

ARA

53

The Italians believed that Asmara would become the administrative center for larger Italian colonial ambitions in the Horn of Africa. The city was well planned and built in the Roman style. Much of the old Italian part of the city is still in excellent condition. In the 1940s Asmara was regarded as one of the cleanest and most beautiful cities in Africa. Under thirty years of Ethiopian occupation, the city was allowed to deteriorate, but it still retains its essential beauty; and since coming under Eritrean control in 1991 it has been undergoing a rapid improvement in infrastructure, building repairs and repainting. Fortunately it did not suffer any direct damage due to the war. It is already one of the cleanest cities in Africa and many Western cities would be shamed by the comparison.

The day begins early in Asmara with the first call to prayer of the muezzin from the tower of Asmara's main mosque. Not long afterwards the massive bells of the Catholic Cathedral chime the beginning of the Christian day while the Orthodox Church celebrates early morning mass. In a world characterized by religious conflict, Christians, Muslims and others have lived peacefully together in this region for centuries.

While remnants of the old Asmara are still to be found, the Italian-built city dominates now, overlain with an Eritrean atmosphere. Asmara is without question one of the most pleasant cities in Africa. Virtually everything in the city can be reached by walking: indeed walking is the best way to see Asmara. Its turn-of-the-century buildings, palm-lined main street, public fountains and the myriad of jacaranda trees and bougainvillaea make it a city to walk in.

Coffee originated in this part of the world and, in addition to the elaborate and time-consuming elegance of the traditional Eritrean coffee service, one of Asmara's basic sounds is the hissing of expresso machines, some of them 30 or 40 years old. Although coffee is an essential part of Eritrean café life, tea is the national drink. Most of it comes from Kenya and has a distinct reddish color. When brewed at home, spices such as cloves or cardamom are often added. A glass of tea is very inexpensive (30-50 local cents: 5-10 US cents). It is served hot, in small glasses with two heaping teaspoons of sugar put into the glass before the tea is added. Those who drink sweet tea stir; those who prefer less sweet don't. It is possible to ask for tea without sugar and Eritrean cafés are conditioning themselves, more or less, to this odd request.

TOURIST INFORMATION & SERVICES

Eritrean Tour Service
Harnet Street No. 61. Tel: 119999.
ETS provides tours, guides and/or transportation for individuals and groups. Virtually any part of the country can be visited using their services. They also offer inexpensive package tours to Massawa. They will pick you up at your hotel and drop you there at the end of the tour. Check with them for current prices and availability of tours.

COMMUNICATIONS

Post Office
The Central Post Office in Asmara is worth a visit. Located two blocks off Harnet Avenue in the center of Asmara on Gennet Heroes Square it was built in the Italian Colonial style and has been virtually perfectly preserved.

The Eritrean postal system is now fully functional and is being improved daily. New stamps were printed for the Eritrean Referendum in April, 1993, the first stamps issued by the new government.

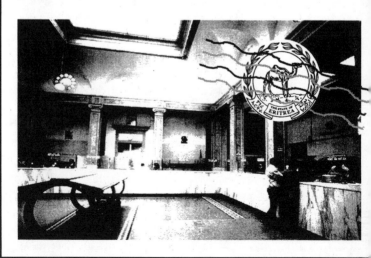

Telephone System
Local Information: 97
International Operator: 98
The Eritrean telephone system is not perfect but it is better than most telephone systems in Africa and it will only become better. Like many services in Eritrea, the telephone system was allowed to deteriorate, especially in the last years prior to the Eritrean military victory in mid-1991. Significant investment is being made in all public services in Eritrea, and the telephone system should soon be of international quality. At present international calls have a 1 minute minimum charge. It is best to inquire about current billing practices. (See page 22 for important information on telephone numbers.)

Telephone bills for private homes and business are prepared with each international call listed by name, date, time, destination and cost.

Fax Services
Fax service is widely available in Asmara, Mendefera, Dekemhare and Massawa and will certainly spread quickly throughout the country as the telephone system improves. Immediately after the end of the war in 1991, when there was no functioning postal system, telephone and fax were the major means of communication. More establishments have a fax than one would expect. Ask if you have to pay a minimum charge for fax time.

Both telephone and fax services were very expensive immediately after the Eritrean victory but prices are falling. The Post Office Tele Communications (corner of Harnet Street and street of Ambasoira Hotel) also offers fax services and was promising cheaper rates and streamlined service; worth inquiring.

Express Services
DHL
The international express shipping firm DHL operates in Asmara. This is a subsidiary of Mitchell Cotts Eritrea. They are located on Emperor Yohannes Street. #50 Tel: 113021, 111494, 111495. P.O. Box 1212. Open 8-12; 14:00-1700. They pick up and deliver. The staff know their

business and are efficient and eager to help; enquire about up to da
information.

Typical rates: Documents up to 500 grammes: 200 birr.

Non-documents up to 500 grammes: 300 birr.

Maximum weight 32 kg.

Another courier service, TNT International, has also set up a bran
office. As we go to press, Federal Express has also started operating
Asmara.

BANKING

The major banks are located on Harnet Street. There is also a ba
next to the Nyala Hotel. They follow the same opening hours as t
government offices. The banks and the government owned hotels a
the only agencies legally entitled to exchange currency.

GOVERNMENT OFFICES

These are located across the street from the National Museum in a la
block of white offices with an imposing front staircase and flower bee
Many ministries are located there but others are scattered througho
central Asmara. In an attempt to relieve the housing shortage in Asma
and to stimulate development outside of the capital, some ministri
will be relocated to other Eritrean towns. The Ministry of Agricultu
will be located in Mendefera while the Ministry of Marine Resourc
and Fisheries will shift to Massawa. A current list of Governme
Offices and their telephone numbers can be found on page 101.

THE UNIVERSITY

The University of Asmara is located about a ten minute walk from t
Government Offices. It was originally founded in 1958 as the "H
Family" University Institute by the Missionary Congregation "Piae Mat
Nigritiae" of the Comboni Sisters. Italian was the language
instruction. In 1960 it was accredited by the Superior Council of
Institute of Italian Universities in accordance with the Gene
Convention governing international academic standards. In 1964
changed its name to the University of Asmara and adopted English as
language of instruction alongside Italian. Eventually English replac
Italian in 1975. In 1977 it came under the Ethiopian Commission
Higher Education and was eventually dismantled in 1990. Its facu
staff, students and moveable property were relocated to Ethiopia.

In 1991 it was refounded as an autonomous university and in 1992 granted a charter guaranteeing its autonomy and academic freedom by the Provisional Government of Eritrea .

The University currently has the Colleges of Science, Arts and Language Studies, Business and Economics, Agriculture and Aquatic Sciences, as well as the Engineering Program, the Education Program and Law Program. The IRD or Institute of Research and Development, located in downtown Asmara near the central Post Office, has been established to promote basic and applied research in all fields.

Currently the University has approximately 2,000 day students and 1,200 evening students.

LIBRARIES

The Municipal Library
82 Ras Alula Street, (near the large Shell Station in the Mai Jah-Jah area), Tel: 12-0738.
Supported by the United States Information Service, the library has a good book collection, some magazines. No fee.

Islamic Learning Centre
Next to the main mosque, on Mosque Square.
Mostly arabic language books, magazines and newspapers, but also some European language materials, including translations of the Koran. The library is a major source of information on Islamic law.

Alliance Francaise
1171 Harnet Avenue, Tel: 12-6599.
Source for French language materials: books, magazines, newspapers. French language courses. Video Club with both French and English language videos. Small café. Offers Tigrinya courses for foreigners. Fee for membership.

The British Council Library
Lorenzo Tazaz Street (near Bar Vittoria)
Tel: 12-3415 or 12-6498,
Books and videos can be borrowed. Up to date magazines. Small membership fee.

NEWSPAPERS-MAGAZINES

Haddas Eritrea, (New Eritrea) appears each Wednesday and Saturday in Tigrinya and Arabic.

Eritrea Profile, an English language weekly appears on Saturday. Both local and international subscriptions are available to *Eritrea Profile.*

International magazines are available in Asmara. One of the major sources is the Awget Bookstore on Harnet Avenue but other shops, especially stationery shops and some grocery shops also sell newpapers and magazines.

EMERGENCIES

1. Police
Day: 11-2811   Night: 11-5555

The main police station in Asmara is located on Victory Street a few doors down from the Keren Hotel. If you need to contact the police it is probably best to do this through your hotel.

2. Medical
Ambulance (Red Cross): 12-2244

Asmara has a number of government hospitals, the Central Hospital, Makane Hiwot, being the most extensive and well equipped. There is also an Italian Hospital. Most embassies can provide up-to-date lists of private doctors and dentists.

3. Fire Department: 11-7777

4. Embassies
A full list of foreign embassies and consulates with their addresses and telephone numbers can be found on page 108.

ACCOMODATIONS

Asmara is undergoing a very rapid program of improvement of tourist accommodations, most of which had been neglected and virtually unused during the 30 years of Ethiopian occupation. Building reconstuction and beautification is underway virtually everywhere in the city. The following offers an idea of the types and costs of accommodation. The larger hotels offer rooms with different levels of comfort (1st, 2nd, 3rd class), usually meaning whether or not there is a toilet and shower in the room. The prices follow accordingly. It is common for guests to inspect the room being offered before accepting it.

All of the hotels listed here are in the central area of Asmara, within walking distance of one another, government offices and shopping.

All hotels charge 10% tax, and add a 10% service fee to the prices listed below. Hotel bills at government-owned hotels (most of those listed here) must be paid in hard currency and prices are usually quoted in US dollars. Hotels are also authorized to change currency. The Government owns the major hotels at present--- taken over from the Dergue which nationalized virtually all property-- but is anxious to privatize them.

Interestingly, no hotel in Asmara has a swimming pool. Eritrea had virtually no international tourist industry for nearly thirty years and there is a need for staff training, catering improvement and upgrading of infrastructure--all of which are underway.

Reservations are highly suggested for all the larger hotels, especially in the summer months when many Eritreans living abroad visit Asmara. If requesting reservatons by fax you need the international prefex for fax (as well as telephone) is: +291-1 plus the number in Asmara. Thus a call to the Ambasoira Hotel would be: (your international access code) 291-1-123222.

ARA

First Class

Ambasoira Hotel
P.O. Box 181
Dejatch Hailu Street, No. 32.
Telephone: 12-3222, Fax: 12-25-95

Modern, first class hotel, with an international clientele. Located in the most prosperous part of Asmara among government offices, consulates and the some of the nicest homes, the Ambasoira is probably the best hotel in Asmara in terms of services. This is the hotel most used by the large international financial and aid organizations and businessmen. It is the place to meet the movers and shakers, the newly prosperous and those on expense accounts. Reservations imperative. Restaurant and Bar. Fax service. Room telephones.

	Single	Double
1st class room:	$49	$66
2nd class room:	$40	$53

Hamasein Hotel
P.O. Box 181
Dejatch Hailu Street, No. 30.
Telephone: 12-3411, 12-3637 No fax.

Next to the Ambasoira, the Hamasein was completely renovated in mid-1993, retaining its original atmosphere. The hotel building is colonial Italian and offers a more charming alternative to the modern Ambasoira but the hotel has had management problems. First class rooms include television (virtually all programming in Tigrinya except CNN twice a week), refrigerator. Room telephones.

	Single	Double
Suites:	$70	$93
1st class room:	$40	$53

Selam Hotel
P.O. Box 867
Telephone: 12-7244, Fax: 12-0662

The Selam Hotel was completely renovated in mid-1993. It offers the same facilities as the Hamasien. Business Center. The best conference facilities in Asmara. Room telephones.

	Single	Double
1st class room:	$70	$92
2nd class room:	$40	$53

Nyala Hotel
P.O. Box 867
Address: Martyrs Avenue
Telephone: 12-31-11, Fax: 12-3111

A modern, high rise hotel with full services--restaurants, bar; not quite as nice as the Ambasoira. Restaurants include the national food restaurant which offers Eritrean cuisine in a modern hotel atmosphere. First class rooms include private bath-shower. Enquire about facilities for second and third class rooms. Some room telephones.

Prices:	Single	Double
1st class room:	$33	$43
2nd class room	$16	$21

64 Middle Class

Ambassador Hotel
P.O. Box 73, Asmara
Address: Harnet Avenue
Telephone: 12-6544, Fax: 11-6545

A modern hotel, located on Harnet Street right in the middle of town, opposite the Catholic Church. A rather pleasant restaurant one floor above the entrance; bar-lounge.

Prices:	Single	Double
1st class room:	$16	$21
2nd class room	$14	$19

Expo Hotel and Sauna
Telephone: 18-1967
A modern hotel which requires a taxi or car to reach the city center. Very popular restaurant.

Prices:	Single	Double
1st class room:	110 birr	165 birr

Keren Hotel
P.O. Box 181, Asmara
Telephone: 12-0740
Address: Victory Street No. 7
The Keren is an old, Italian built hotel which retains some of its turn of the century character. The rooms are simple, clean and even the 3rd

class rooms (sink only) are more than satisfactory for travelers. The nicest dining room in Asmara. Restaurant and bar service. Government buildings virtually next door.

Prices:	*Single*	*Double*
1st class room:	**$16**	**$19**
2nd class room:	**$14**	**$16**

Legesse Hotel
Address: Ras Beyene Beraki St. No. 42
Telephone: 12-5054

All the taxi drivers will know it. Privately owned. Much nicer inside than it appears from the outside. Shared bathrooms. Includes a bar and good restaurant. Increasingly popular.
Double: **55 birr**
Single: **33 birr**

Lower Middle Class

Zegereda/Rose Hotel
Tel: 113864

On Senafe Street behind Cinema Dante one block behind Harnet Avenue.

A room is 20 birr per night. Rooms are simple and clean. Toilets and showers are available but not in the rooms. No restaurant but a small bar attached serving tea, beer, soft drinks. Very friendly and helpful. Restaurants and snackbars nearby.

There are a number of small hotels and many pensions in Asmara; many of them excellent value. This is an area of accomodation which is expanding and improving very rapidly as peace and stabilty encourage investment.

Camping
A cautionary note. While camping is not prohibited in Eritrea it is not a good idea unless accompanied by a local resident. During the war countless landmines were laid by opposing forces and while an active program of removal is underway straying off known routes is potentially dangerous. At present there is no camping facility in Asmara or Massawa.

ERITREAN FOOD

Eritrea Profile, the English language weekly newspaper, has a restaurant column. The restaurant business is expanding rapidly in Eritrea; food, service and variety are changing almost daily. This is the best place to keep up with new restaurant openings.

Eritrea has two main food traditions, its indigenous tradition which has many variations (depending on whether one is in the highlands or lowlands) and Italian cuisine. Most restaurants serve both.

The food of Asmara reflects the highland Eritrean tradition and is based on a variety of sauces and stews eaten with *injera*, a large sourdough pancake made of *t'aff* (an indigenous grain), sorghum or occasionally maize.

Tsebhi, which is also called *zigni,* is a stew made from chicken, beef or lamb. It is simmered for hours, traditionally in clay pots, in a tomato sauce spiced with *berberé* chili powder and other spices. *Tibsi* or *qkoolewaa* is a meat sauté prepared with lamb or beef, fresh tomatoes and hot peppers. Most Eritreans cannot afford a meat-based diet and they eat *shiro*, a chickpea porridge made in many different ways, with *injera. Birsen* is a lentil curry. *Alitcha* is a curried vegetable stew ,with or without meat.

There are many other Eritrean specialties and the Government is encouraging more use of fish which is inexpensive and abundant in Eritrea, but these are the major dishes to be found in restaurants.

Tea, is called *shahi.* If you order coffee or *boon* you will get expresso. *Machiatto* is a stronger form of cappuccino. Some people prefer to drink either *machiatto latte* or pure hot milk.Most of the hotels have restaurants that offer simple to full meals. Many restaurants have Eritrean dishes in the kitchen but not on the menu. Ask about them if you are interested. Prices are more than reasonable and the quality of food is good and almost always freshly prepared.

Water

Water should be boiled before drinking. Many people prefer to drink mineral water. Real mineral water is bottled in Asmara under strictly controlled health and sanitation regulations and is widely available in restaurants, cafés and markets. A half litre bottle costs about 1.50 birr. Ask for *mai gaz*. It is supposed to be lightly carbonated but sometimes is not when CO_2 is unavailable (by-product of beer brewing at the Asmara brewery), or when the corking machine doesn't get the seal right. Bottles of mineral water, as well as all other bottled drinks, will be opened before your eyes. It is also possible to buy uncarbonated mineral water: ask for *mai*.

RESTAURANTS

New restaurants will be opening with regularity in Asmara as tourist demand increases. A few suggestions:

Keren Hotel Restaurant
The newly named Keren Hotel was originally called the Albergo Italia and was Asmara's finest hotel. It was built in 1899 and its dining room retains much of its original charm. In addition to the main dining room it has two smaller rooms for groups of 6-10. The dining room is open for breakfast, lunch and dinner.

The menu usually includes three or four soups, salads, Italian specialities and a variety of fish and steaks as well as chicken.

The St. George Restaurant
Fesshaie Kifle Street 34
The simple menu in this rather charming restaurant is in Tigrinya, Italian and English. As in many restaurants Italian food is an option with Spaghetti, Lasagna and other Italian specialties offered (but not always available) in addition to steak, chicken, sheep's head and other entrées. The Eritrean Fisheries Department is making serious efforts to make refrigerated daily deliveries of Red Sea fish to Asmara and these are widely offered on restaurant menus. Soups and first courses are priced at 7 birr while main courses are 8 birr. Beer, locally bottled carbonated mineral water, local wines and soft drinks are available.

Asmara Restaurant
The Asmara Restaurant, on the side of the main Post Office, serves both Italian and Eritrean food. It is very popular and seems to get better with each visit. Its simple, main dining room has only six-eight tables but a small door in the main room leads to a small second eating area. The kitchen has been recently refurbished and the Asmara intends to be the first to offer fresh shellfish--shrimp and lobster. Prices are in the lower range.

Beilul Restaurant
Across and up the street from the Nyala Hotel. Very simple, serving Eritrean food. Very popular with Eritreans, especially for its zilzil (12 birr), barbecued meat served with a charcoal brazier to keep it hot. A usual meal would be injera, zilzil, salad, beer. A dinner for two with zilzil and beer costs about 40 birr.

Bologna Restaurant and Hotel, Tel: 18-9360
The Bologna is very popular and is less fancy than the Expo Restaurant located around the corner. Tablecloths, napkins, and like most Eritrean restaurants, good service.

The Bologna Restaurant serves Italian food, most served as generous portion first courses followed by second meat-based courses. The Bologna offers tongue, kidneys, and tripe in addition to steaks.

The Bologna serves in an Eritrean-Italian manner; warm bread is brought to the table, a bottle of local mineral water is automatically opened unless you say no.

Caravel Restaurant and Hotel, Tel: 12-3830
Drive past the Nyala Hotel on Martyrs' Avenue to the roundabout; around it until facing the street which leads up the hill. The popular and busy Caravel is on the left side of the street.

Some say this is the best pizza in Asmara; good local and Ethiopian wines.

Castello Restaurant, Tel: 12-0453
Located in a residental section of Asmara on Godana Dej. Zerom Kifle. Taxi drivers will probably know the way, but ask first. As the name suggests, Italian food mixed with some Eritrean specialities. Many people go to Castello to eat the canneloni, Most entrees cost 10 birr. One of the better wine lists in Asmara. What Castello lacks in atmosphere it makes up in the food it serves. One of the few restaurants where it is possible to sit outside..

Expo Restaurant, Hotel and Sauna Bath, Tel: 18-1967
The Expo Restaurant, Hotel and (yes) Sauna. All the taxi drivers know it but be certain you specify Expo Restaurant and not the Expo Exhibition Grounds. Off of the airport road: best to enquire for directions. The Bologna Restaurant is nearby.

This is a modern hotel and restaurant frequented by civil servants, the new entrepreneurs, diplomats and development workers. The food is good, the decor pleasant, prices are reasonable and the service is excellent. It has a small but adequate menu with soups and pasta dishes serving as first courses (9-15 birr). Various meat dishes including T Bone Steak (12 birr), are offered as second courses. Desserts include creme caramel, fresh fruit cocktail and ice cream (all 4 birr).

Pizzaria Napoli, Tel: 12-3784
Many Eritreans lived in exile during the war, some of them in Italy. Pizzaria Napoli offers the greatest selection of pizza in Asmara. They prepare for take-away and also do special pizza orders. Near Bar Vittoria.

The Nyala Hotel Restaurant, on the 7th floor of the Nyala Hotel specializes in Eritrean food served in a traditional decor. It is an excellent place to try Eritrean cuisine in a modern atmosphere.

Restaurant of the Ambassador Hotel is one floor up with a view over Harnet Avenue and the Cathedral. Eritrean foods plus pasta and variety of meats.

Re'esee Ketema, a neighborhood restaurant located, as its name implies, "at the head of the city" opposite the large stadium at the end of Harnet Street (turn right, walk to the sign which is in Tigrinya but also says "Restaurant" in English). Re'esee Ketema, which is owned by two sisters, looks like a bar and you must walk through the bar into the dining room. If the small dining room is full keep going, there is another small eating area. The lasagna is among the best in Asmara.

Legesse Hotel Restaurant, Tel: 12-5054. In downtown Asmara at 42 Ras Beyene Beraki Street. Modern dining room with a predominantly Italian-style menu. They don't always have everything on the menu but the service is willing and the food is good. They offer a number of alterative entrees such as eggplant parmigano as well as an excellent lentil soup. Prices in the 10 birr per entree range. Definitely worth a try.

Sudanese Restaurants
Sudanese restaurants are scattered throughout Asmara. Most serve, in addition to various meat and fish dishes, the two basic Sudanese dishes, foule (dark cooked beans prepared in a variety of ways) and bamiya, (okra cooked in oil with spices). Usually served with fresh rolls or *injera*. Rice and salad usually available.

Tipping Etiquette

Hotels automatically add a 15% service charge. Some restaurants sometimes add a 10% service charge; others do not. It will be indicated on the bill. In cafes, where you often pay at the cash register prior to ordering tips are not usual unless you have not paid in advance. Often there is a small tip dish near the cash register. In restaurants 10% is adequate.

BUYING FOOD

Tired of eating in restaurants?

Although there are many small grocery shops in Asmara, two shops are are especially recommended if you would like to buy for lunch or for general shopping. One is on Harnet Street 114. Good selection of breads, locally made ham, vegetables. It has a particularly good selection of local and imported items including wines.

The other is on the roundabout at Piazza Tambien. Both sell the excellent Asmara made provolone cheese (100 grams for 3 birr). Fresh, locally-made mozzarella and ricotta are usually available. The Parmesan is imported and expensive. Locally made mortadella is also available and excellent.

On the same roundabout is a small leather goods shop offering well made, very inexpensive smaller items: wallets, bags, eye-glasses cases.

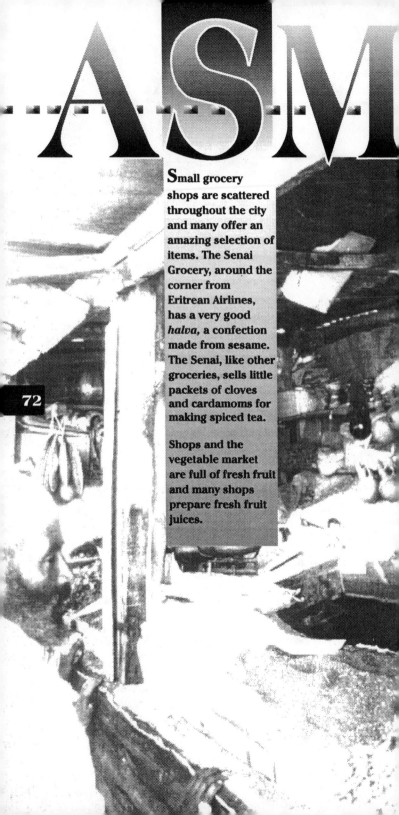

Small grocery shops are scattered throughout the city and many offer an amazing selection of items. The Senai Grocery, around the corner from Eritrean Airlines, has a very good *halva,* a confection made from sesame. The Senai, like other groceries, sells little packets of cloves and cardamoms for making spiced tea.

Shops and the vegetable market are full of fresh fruit and many shops prepare fresh fruit juices.

ARA

WHAT TO SEE IN ASMARA

The National Museum

Built by the Italians 70 years ago in the Roman and Florentine styles as the residence for the Governor of Eritrea, it was subsequently used by the British and the Ethiopians. This was the former palace and grounds of Emperor Haile Selassie. The Emperor maintained palaces in each of the provinces of Ethiopia (Eritrea was annexed by Ethiopia as a "province" in 1962) as a symbol of power but he personally rarely visited them.

The buildings include his former palace, the houses of his important civil and domestic servants, the former aviary, tennis courts, and the garages where he kept his automobiles (two of which---1950s Cadillacs---have remained in pristine condition) and his personal chapel.

The Eritrean government has spent considerable effort to restore the former palace after twenty years of neglect. The gardens, beautifully manicured with sculpted bushes, a fountain and a rich bird life, have been restored. The grounds alone are worth a visit. Admission fee: 2 birr.

Photography

You will have to pay a 50 birr fee to bring a video camera into the grounds; still photography is not permitted in the museum buildings.

The main building contains the Archaeology Museum, with its collection of artifacts dating back to Greek and Roman times. There is also a small collection of ancient Orthodox scrolls written in Ge'ez, the alphabet still used today in Eritrea and Ethiopia. The collection is small but worth seeing since it gives an overview of early Eritrean societies from many parts of the country. No doubt the collection will expand and be improved in the coming years.

Red arrows guide you down to the Ethnographic Museum. Here you will find the traditional dress, weaponry, domestic implements and jewellery of the nine Eritrean nationalities. One of the displays shows the type of house built by each nationality. These displays are constructed in what were formerly tiny prison cells, each of which contained up to 15 prisoners, during the Ethiopian occupation. One cell is identified as such and contains examples of handcuffs, whips,

Ethnographic Museum is the Military Museum. You can't miss it; outside is a large collection of mostly Soviet supplied military equipment captured from the Ethiopians.

Eritreans fought a 30 year war of liberation against Ethiopia and suffered over 65,000 dead as a result. The museum is a monument to those who died and to those who survived. There is much to see in the museum, including displays of materials produced by the underground workshops in the Eritrean base area of Orota. Of particular interest are examples of the locally made spare parts which kept captured weaponry functioning. It is this spirit of self-reliance that sustained the struggle and will be of critical importance in Eritrea's future development.

THE MARKETS

Asmara's markets (the "Shuk") are more than worth visiting. They are divided into the covered vegetable market, the nearby market selling spices and dried vegetables and grains, the covered furniture and second hand clothing market next to the handicraft market (behind the main Mosque) where only locally produced items are for sale and Medeber, sometimes called the recycling market (which also has many grinding mills for spices and grains), where virtually every bit of scrap metal ends up pounded, folded, soldered and welded into new items.

The marketeers are friendly and eager to sell; don't hesitate to walk around. They will make you a special tourist price; don't be afraid to haggle---they expect it. A simple greeting "Salaam" will work wonders.

In the region of the markets are many street vendors, especially between the Orthodox Cathedral and Medeber, who sell enamel pots and pans, rubber sandals of every type, including the fighters' sandals. During the struggle each fighter, from the current President to the newest recruit, wore black rubber sandals. These were made in an underground workshop. The sandals were not particularly beautiful but they were sturdy and one needed tough feet to wear them since they were made of half new-rubber and half recycled rubber from old sandals that had been granulated. Now you can buy soft, 100% new rubber sandals, but they are going out of fashion with those who can afford better shoes as too many Eritreans wore them for too many years out of necessity.

PLACES OF WORSHIP

Jamie al-Khulafa'e al-Rashidin Mosque

The green and white Jamie al-Khulafa'e al-Rashidin Mosque is located on Mosque Place, a few blocks away from the City Hall. Its tower will guide you there. Men are free to enter after taking off their shoes. Photography is permitted but should be done with discretion and respect for a house of God.

The call to prayer from the tower of Jamie al-Khulafa'e al-Rashidin Mosque can be heard five times a day, everywhere in Asmara.

Enda Mariam (St. Mary's) Orthodox Christian Church

Is on the hill at the eastern end of the city. It is a recognizable part of the city's skyline. Although the church location is quite old, the current church is relatively new.

In front of, and to the left of the church, in the large open area, you will see several stones hanging from a metal support. Take one of the small stones from on top of the support and tap the larger ones--these were the original church bells. The low buildings at the entrance to the Church are part of the Orthodox Christian Church school.

You may enter the church but be aware that there are separate doors for men and for women. Men enter on the left and women on the right. Inside, men worship on the left side and women on the right half. It is also customary to remove one's shoes just inside the door. Photography is also permitted but again, it is a house of God, and you are asked to dress appropriately, and photograph with discretion. The church contains some fine example of Orthodox religious painting.

Our Lady of the Rosary Cathedral
Located on Harnet Street, the Franciscan Cathedral, built in the 1920s, with its imposing bell tower, dominates the centre of the city, as it was inteded to do. It is possible to climb the bell tower whose clock still functions and whose bells ring on the hour.

Originally planned as the centre of Roman Catholicism for the region, the brick complex is built in a beautiful renaissance style, patterned after an Italian cloister. The complex contains the Cathedral, a school and printing facilities.

TSETSERAT

Locally called the "tank graveyard" it is located on the western side of the Denden (formerly the American and later Ethiopian Kagnew) military base. It is a junkyard of destroyed arms, tanks, armoured personnel carriers, artillery left behind by the army of the Dergue, the previous military government of Ethiopia.

You are free to visit and photograph at Tsetserat (any taxi driver can take you there). It is a sobering testament to the price Eritreans paid for their independence.

CINEMAS AND OPERA HOUSE

Asmara has a surprising number of large cinemas, all built during the Italian period. If you are a fan of old cinemas they are worth a visit. The Impero, Asmara, Roma and Odeon are good examples, although they suffered from a lack of maintenance during the occupation.

The cinemas remain one of the most popular forms of entertainment: main floor seats are 2 birr, the balcony costs 3 birr.

The Opera House, once the site of touring company performances, is to be found on Harnet Street, next to the telecommunications building. It too, has been neglected over the past thirty years, but has already played host to concerts.

COFFEE & CAFÉS

Coffee originated in the Kaffa highlands of Ethiopia, where it is still a major crop. Coffee is also grown in Eritrea, especially in the Semienawi Bahri area, and if you are lucky enough to be invited to an Eritrean home for coffee, it is an experience you will be unlikely to forget. The whole ceremony can take hours and begins with the roasting of the beans--each participant seeming to have their own idea of just how much, or how little they should be roasted. At the critical moment the pan with the smoking beans is passed around and one fans the smoke so as to appreciate the aroma of the freshly roasted beans. Then comes pounding in a mortar and pestle, and then the brewing, usually in a hand-made clay pot over a charcoal brazier, carefully allowing the coffee to boil briefly three times.

Coffee is served in thimble-sized cups with lots of sugar. After the first round which is the strongest, the pot is refilled with water and then a second round is prepared and then a third, after which it is considered too weak to drink. If you really like coffee, this is for you. During The Struggle, the occasions when coffee was available were virtually the only times one caught a glimpse of normal Eritrean society, when the punishing day-to-day hardships of war seemed to recede.

Cafés are still the center of social life in Asmara. You will find them everywhere. People tend not to linger in cafés as is customary in Europe, but everyone who can visits the cafés. Like their Italian counterparts upon which they were modeled, they offer a full range of coffee, cappuccino, macchiato (stronger cappuccino), teas and alcoholic drinks. Unlike their Italian counterparts they are inexpensive. At present they offer no tables outside, except at City Park.

A cappuccino (if you don't want sugar in it say so when ordering---the same with tea) costs about .60 birr, a donut .50 birr. Many cafés also offer freshly baked cakes, cookies, biscuits and donuts. They also serve a range of aperitifs such as Zibib (an anise flavored liquor like ouso or anisette), Mentha (a menthe liquor), whiskies, gins, cocktail mixes and soft drinks. Asmara beer is brewed in an immaculate brewery in Asmara. The Asmara brewery also makes the liquors. Many cafés continue the Italian gelatto or ice cream tradition.

It is not possible to list all of the cafés in Asmara; here are just a few you might wish to try:

Bar Vittoria
Itegue Zehaitu Street 18, near the National Museum, City Park and main government offices--a favorite of government officials. Good baked items, ice cream and friendly service. Fresh donuts in the morning.

City Park Café
In the City Park next to the National Museum. A pavilion offering outside seating. Good bakery in the same area as well as ice cream.

Royal Café
On Harnet Avenue. Very popular with people working in the nearby offices for after-lunch coffee and drinks. Always lots of people at peak times.

Café Impero
On the main street in the center of Asmara next to the Impero cinema. Always busy, offering a full range services, including bakery goods and ice cream.

Bar Trestelle
Opposite the Red Sea Pension and Agip Station at the far end of Victory Street on the roundabout. Popular with car owners: pull up, beep and someone will take your order and bring your cappuccino to the car.

LUNCHES-SNACK BARS

The Cathedral Snack Bar opposite, what else, the Cathedral on Harnet Avenue, offers a variety of fresh fruit drinks (guava, papaya and banana---all to recommend), bottled soft drinks, tea and coffee.

The menu is only in Tigrinya but offers standard Eritrean snack foods: fried egg and tomato sandwich, "hamburger" which is actually a thin slice of fried steak on a roll (very good) and others. The waiters will tell you what's available.

SHOPPING-GIFTS

Leather Goods

Fine leather work is done in Asmara. Some of the larger manufacturing leather shops are near the silversmiths on Itague Zaihatu Street (at the top of the street is Bar Vittoria).

The Asmara Sweater Factory has recently started making leather jackets (cowhide or sheepskin) for both local sale and export. The hides come from Eritrea, Ethiopia and Sudan and are tanned and dyed locally. They have a considerable stock of sizes and styles. Like most of the shops they will make a jacket to size in a few days and even modify the design to your liking. Specify with or without insulation. Expect to pay between 450-550 birr for a half length or jacket style. Their jackets are for sale in shops on Harnet Street or at the factory, Christopher de Gama Street No. 131. (Upstairs). Tel: 112904. Asmara craftsmen make leather bags, wallets, belts, glasses cases, and leather jackets. Prices range from 100-150 birr for truly elegant bags.

Shoes

Handmade shoes are available in Asmara. On Harnet Street 86, next to the Cathedral Snack Bar you will find the shop of Neguse G. If you like Italian-inspired design interpreted by Eritrean sensitivities and made in Asmara, don't miss Neguse G. The price is 150 birr. If you have a week, they will make them to order. They import the soles but the shoes are made in Asmara on Italian lasts; they fit. They have a surprising range of shoes from sandals to loafers to elegant dress shoes.

Gold and Silversmiths

There is a rich and elegant tradition of silversmithing in Eritrea and the surrounding regions stemming from the Islamic and Orthodox Christian traditions. Silverwork is widely found in Asmara and other Eritrean cities and towns; gold less so. Designs tend to be similar in all of the shops but each has its own signature. Rings, earrings, Orthodox crosses and bracelets predominate. Gold and silver items are sold by weight. Expect to pay between 4 and 5 birr per gram for silver. Many of the old silver pieces are actually made from large silver coins. The early favorite was the Austro-Hungarian Maria Theresa dollar which silversmiths often still sell. There is also a silver look-alike which has a slight pale yellow metallic look due to a high percentage of nickel (locally called "nikka") or copper. It is clearly distinguishable from purer silver when the two are laid side by side. Some beautiful work is done with this metal and these pieces are sold generally as pieces, not by weight.

Silversmiths are located all over the city but concentrated on Itague Zaihatu Street and near the main mosque on Said Bekri El Morgany St. The latter tend to have more old silver pieces. In some shops you have to ask for old silver since silversmiths are rightly proud of their own manufactures and feature them in the window.

Handicraft Market

The local market has a section solely for handicrafts--these items are for local consumption, not for tourists: clay coffee pots, handmade rope, charcoal braziers, baskets, cosmetic containers, spices. If you look carefully you will find stands selling bottle caps full of crystal-like substances--many of these are incense, to be thrown into the fire while making coffee. If you come from the Catholic tradition you will immediately recognize the smell from church: frankincense and myhrr.

ARA····

NIGHTLIFE & MUSIC

In addition to regular special events such as discos and live bands (widely advertised in Asmara), there are a number of bars and night spots, perhaps the best known of which is located in the basement of the Asmara Theatrical Society on Harnet Avenue.

Arts

An increasing number of organizations have display space where photographs, paintings, sculpture and other arts are displayed. Usually these are announced with affiches around the city.

Sports

Eritreans are very sports minded but had little opportunity to develop sports under Ethiopian occupation. That has all changed now.

The national football (soccer) team won first place in a regional competition on its first time out, beating far more experienced teams. The Asmara football stadium seats 55,000. Seats costs between 2-5 birr. Games are played with intense competition and great spirit as football develops as the national sport.

If you are out in the countryside early in the morning you might see the Eritrean bicycle clubs practising---flying by on their elegant Italian racing bicycles wearing the latest racing jerseys and shorts. Bicycle racing takes place on most weekends.

Once a year Asmara hosts an automobile-motorcycle race run on the city streets in the town center. If you are fortunate enough to be there for the race don't miss it. This is not the slick, highly commercial automobile racing done in Europe; the cars are used on a daily basis and prepared just for this race by local mechanics. You will see amateur racing at its best.

ONE DAY TRIPS FROM ASMARA

Visitors to Asmara who have access to a car can make a number of interesting day trips.

Keren
The town of Keren is the provincial capital of Senhit Province and one of the major agricultural centers of Eritrea, particularly for fruits and vegetables. The drive to Keren is very beautiful passing through a variety of landscapes. Near Keren one passes through the Elaberiet agricultural center, one of the most productive in the country. Irrigated by a series of seven dams, Elaberiet produces fruits and vegetables for Asmara and other markets. In addition, its dairy herds supply fresh milk, butter and the cheeze factory produces provolone and other cheezes. Keren itself is in the center of one of Eritrea's main fruit growing regions.

The Keren Hotel, located in the center of the town offers simple but clean accomodation.

Serejeka--Zager and Sobur--Murara
On the Keren road is the agricultural community of Serejeka and the hill villages of Weki and Zager. This is an area where the resistance to Ethiopian domination developed early in the EPLF period and the villages of this area contributed many of their sons and daughters to the liberation movement and suffered many losses. Like many villages in Eritrea they have built a monument to their fallen children. One drives in the direction of the town of Keren and at Serejeka, where there is a market, and where one can buy fresh fruits and vegetables and eat a fried egg sandwich on a fresh roll in one of the thatched eating places (or drink suwa, the national beer-like beverage). At Serejeka the road to Keren makes a large turn to the left but just at this point is an earthen road going straight ahead which leads into the hill villages of the Zager area. You need a 4 wheel drive vehicle for the trip, not because 4 wheel drive is necessary but sometimes clearance under the car can be critical.

There is no particular site to visit or place to see; the journey is the reason for making the trip. There are no restaurants and no cafes; this is rural Eritrea, the way most Eritreans live. Few foreigners visit the area.

The road climbs to the top of hills and then begins a winding descent, down the escarpment. If you continue down the road, eventually it will split, the ascending road to the left leads to Murara, an agricultural area where much of Eritrea's coffee is grown. The road descending to the right leads to the farming region of Sobur (from Serejeka the trip to Sobur takes about an hour). At first the area is typically dry highland Eritrea but as you enter the micro climate of the Sobur area it becomes lusciously green with terraced fields. Sobur is a perfect place for a picnic.

If you continue down the escarpment the temperature rises and eventually becomes quite warm and tropical. The road is said to continue to Ghinda, on the Asmara-Massawa road, but the last stretch runs through river beds and can be difficult to find.

Mendefera
Mendefera is the capital of Seraye Province and a market town about 1 hour's drive from Asmara. The town itself is typical of provincial Eritrea. Of special interest are the many small shops in the older part of the town. There you will find spice merchants, silversmiths and shops selling the necessities for camel caravans. The merchants are friendly, even if you are only looking around or making pictures and they offer the opportunity to buy things which are seldom seen.

The trip to Mendefera descends the escarpment and passes through a variety of landscapes which give a good indication of the rich agricultural potential of this part of Eritrea. Eventually the Ministry of Agriculture will be located in Mendefera. At present Mendefera offers two hotels for tourists, both are located on the road to Adi Quala just as you leave.

MULTI-DAY TRIPS FROM ASMARA

The obvious multi-day trip from Asmara is to Massawa. However, 180 km from Asmara is the ancient town of Axum, in Ethiopia, once the center of a civilization and empire which reached over a wide area of the Horn of Africa. For centuries Axum was the center of Orthodox Christianity in the Horn of Africa. Once a destination for international tourism, Axum was closed to outside visitors during most of the Dergue period after 1974. In 1989, when the Tigrai People's Liberation Front captured Axum from the Ethiopian Government, Axum was superficially damaged by the fighting but is now rebuilding and is once again receiving tourists. The easiest access to Axum is through Eritrea.

Axum is a sacred town and a central historical site for Orthodox Christians (Muslims have also a important presence there). The Orthodox Christian monks of Axum claim to keep the original Ark of the Covenant (the gold-lined box built to keep the two tablets of stone on which the ten commandments were written and given to Moses on Mount Sinai) in the monastery complex of Saint Mary of Zion, a claim which has recently been taken seriously by modern scholars. A copy of the Ark is displayed each year in January during the Timket Ceremony. Ethiopia takes particular pride in Axum and its religious tradition.

Axum offers a number of simple hotels and a luxury hotel is being refurbished after years of neglect. Check with the Ethiopian Embassy in Asmara concerning visa requirements. The Eritrean Tour Service is planning to offer trips to Axum.

The road to Axum passes through Mendefera and Adi Quala where one leaves the plateau and decends into the spectacular valley which separates Eritrea from Ethiopia. Up to the Ethiopian border the road is paved.

Outside of Adi Quala, high on the hill overlooking the valley and Ethiopia in the distance is a mausoleum-monument (Daro Kunaat) built during the Fascist period in Italy honoring the Italian solders and officers killed at the battle of Adua in 1896, Italy's first and unsuccessful attempt to conquer Ethiopia. The road to the monument has all but disappeared into a footpath and is only reachable with four-wheel drive vehicle, although the drive is not particularly difficult. The monument has been cared for since its construction by the inhabitants of a nearby village, who still receive a small stipend from the Italian Government. The Monument looks across the valley to the distant plains near the town of Adua where Italy suffered its defeat. When we visited the monument in 1993 we were the first to sign the guest book since 1974.

SAWA

BASIC FACTS

Massawa is an ancient port on the Red Sea, which today serves as Eritrea's major port. Virtually everything imported by sea into Eritrea comes via Massawa. Assab, Eritrea's other port in the extreme south of the country, was built essentially to service the needs of Ethiopia.

Massawa was badly damaged at the end of the war with Ethiopia when the Dergue bombed the city off and on for months. Facing a massive task of reconstruction, the Massawans are busy rebuilding the city and seeking outside aid to assist in the reconstruction of the architecturally significant buildings, many of which are built of coral blocks.

Massaw replaced the now buried port of Adulis which was once the outlet to the Red Sea for the ancient kingdom of Axum and the earliest trade route in the region. Adulis was part of an archipelago of Red Sea and Indian Ocean ports that included Suakin in Sudan, Beilul in Eritrea, Mogadishu in Somalia, Lamu and Mombasa in Kenya, Pemba and Zanzibar in Tanzania, and others further south which linked the trading networks of the Red Sea, the Gulf and the Indian Ocean.

Over the centuries Massawa has been occupied by the Turks, Egyptians, Italians, British and Ethiopians, out of which it has developed it's "Red Sea" character---a mixture of all of its influences. Although the settlement of Massawa is very old, the current town was built in the late nineteenth century, destroyed by earthquake in 1921 and rebuilt by the Italians in a variety of architectural styles. Old Massawa is one of the most unique towns on the eastern African coast and is certainly worth a visit. Massawa is coolest during "winter" (December to January) when temperatures are more moderate than during the hot season (June to September).

TRAVEL TO MASSAWA

The road to Massawa winds its way down through the mountains from Asmara, roughly paralleling the old railway line. The drive is quite spectacular in places. In the Asmara area the mountains have been terraced and are often covered with cactus introduced into Eritrea by the Italians.

Debre Bizen Monastery

About half an hour by car from Asmara is the small town of Nafasit. On the top of Mt. Bizen overlooking Nafasit is the 700-year old monastery of Debre Bizen. It is possible for men to visit the monastery, but the only way to the make the 400- meter, 7 km climb to the top is on foot. The celibate monks say only men are allowed not because they dislike women; on the contrary they like them too much. The way looks formidable from below but is not difficult or dangerous and depending on your condition takes between one and a half and three hours. A day visit to Debre Bizen is realistic since the best times to make the climb and return are very early morning and late afternoon. Male visitors are encouraged and it is customary to leave the monks a contribution to aid in the maintenance and reconstruction of the monastery. You will be taken to the *Magabe* (the monk responsible for hospitality) upon your arrival as a courtesy. Don't be surprised if the *Magabe* asks you to sit down while students wash your feet: a custom of the monastery since the days of its founder, Abune Phillipos.

The monastery is actually a small village of stone monk's houses, small churches and agricultural support buildings. It has about 60 monks and a fluctuating number of students in its religious school. Once very prosperous, most of the monastery's property was confiscated during the time of the Dergue's occupation, which actively discouraged religious institutions. The monastery is now negotiating with the Government of Eritrea for the return of at least some of their former land and property holdings.

Getting to Massawa from Asmara takes about two-three hours. As the tourist posters proclaim, one really does go through three seasons in three hours: the Fall coolness of Asmara, the Spring like, sometimes lush plateau around Ghinda and finally the Summer heat of the Red Sea Desert which is warm and humid compared to the ideal climate of Asmara. The road is in good condition and literally

getting better each week but it still takes as much time to go down as it does to come back up.

The Eritrean Tour Service offers a package tour with mini bus service and guide. Inquire at their offices.

It is also possible to take the bus (about four hours) which costs 8.50 birr. The old buses are being replaced with new ones and most are now very comfortable. One waits until the bus is full or nearly full and then it departs. It stops along the way and its final destination is the entrance to Old Massawa.

Bus schedules vary and it is wise to check the current schedule but buses travelling in both directions usually leave between 7:00-8:00.

GETTING AROUND MASSAWA

It is possible to walk to virtually every part of Massawa in 30 minutes. There are also buses, taxis and mini-van taxis. Taxis running on fixed routes charge 1 birr. Fix the price before boarding. The taxis and buses stop at the entrance to Old Massawa. There you will also find the bus station (tickets from the driver). Across the street is the Post Office.

The local or Baraka harbor is also by the bus depot where the traditional sailing ships (now virtually all motorized) of the Red Sea and Indian Ocean are moored and where they board cargo and sometimes passengers. Other sailing ships are to be found at the fishing harbor near the Red Sea Hotel.

The boats travel to the other coastal harbors of Eritrea, especially those too small for larger vessels, to the Dhalak Islands (about a six hour journey) and some as far as Saudi Arabia, Yemen and the Gulf---three-four days.

What to see

For tourism purposes Massawa can be divided into Old and New Massawa. Old Massawa is the original part of the city built over centuries with the architectural influences of all those who occupied the town. It was built by seamen, traders and merchants. New Massawa, across the small causeway, was built much later and has a different character, reflecting later Italian influences. This was the center of coastal colonial administration.

The Ministry of Tourism offers a walking tour brochure and map of Old Massawa, which is very useful for visitors. Ask for it at their office. The town is its own attraction and while there are significant buildings, especially near the modern port area, mostly one just browses around the town, taking tea here or there and watching life go by. The people are friendly and inquisitive.

WHERE TO STAY

Massawa is a favorite weekend destination for Eritreans and resident non-Eritreans. Hotel rooms are limited and it is becoming essential to make reservations, particularly for the weekends. At least one new hotel is under construction and some pensions are undergoing renovations.

In Old Massawa
The Dhalak Hotel, with a wonderful location on the harbor, just opposite the entrance to Old Massawa, was once a hotel for American servicemen stationed in Asmara. It was eventually taken over by the Dergue but has been completely renovated during 1993. Telephone: 552725

Prices: vary by type of rooms. In the range of 80 birr per night. Enquire.

There are a number or small hotels and pensions scattered throughout both old and new Massawa which offer accommodations of varying comfort.

In New Massawa
The Red Sea Hotel
Once the premier hotel in Massawa it is located a few minutes taxi ride from Old Massawa directly on the water. The Red Sea was damaged during the war but is being rebuilt. Check with the Eritrean Tour Service for current status and prices.

Other Massawa Hotels which were under construction or refurbishment when we went to press and which are now finished:

Central Hotel, tel: 55-20-02
A privatley owned hotel with good restaurant and patio.

Corallo Hotel, tel: 55-24-06
Privately owned, newly refurbished, large rooms.

Luna Hotel, tel: 55-22-72
Also privately owned. Popular, US motel style.

At the Beach
The Gurgusum Beach Hotel has been completely renovated and enlarged. It is a single story bungalow structure located directly on the beach, about 20 minutes drive from the town center. Rooms are pleasant and include showers, ceiling fans and air conditioning. Price: 84 Birr per night.

The hotel has a restaurant-bar serving Italian and Eritrean food. The tables are decked with tablecloths and cloth napkins.

The Hamasien Hotel
Completed as we went to press. Located a few kilometres from the Gurgusum Beach Hotel, the Hamasien is air conditioned, has conference facilities and will soon have a restaurant.

Camping
Camping is not prohibited but is not recommended due to the possibility of land-mines. The government has a comprehensive program of clearing land-mines but this will take some years before the country can be completely cleansed of this scourge.

RESTAURANTS

In Old Massawa there are a variety of local restaurants. Of special mention is the Eritrea Restaurant. Because Old Massawa has no street signs, the best way to find the Eritrea Restaurant is to start at the Post Office, just at the entrance to the old city, and follow the main street for two or three blocks until coming to the Red Sea Grocery on the left hand side. Look down the narrow street and you will see a sign which simply says "Restaurant" in English.

The Eritrea Restaurant serves traditional Eritrean foods as well as grilled fresh fish, spaghetti, lasagna, grilled meats (all kept fresh in the refrigerators standing around the eating area), fresh salads made of romaine lettuce, tomatoes, onions and chilis. They also offer sandwiches served on freshly baked rolls. The dressing is found in the bottles on the table which have a small hole punched through the cap. They also serve beer and large bottles of mineral water, Eritrean tea and coffee.

Prices: a bottle of mineral water costs 1 birr; the most expensive entrées 6 birr but prices are rising.

At meal times the Eritrea Restaurant is packed but one always seems to find a place. The restaurant is authentic, inexpensive and the service is simple but quick.

One of the best places to eat in Massawa is at the Afar fish restaurant. The Afars live along the coast of Eritrea south of Asmara and are renowned fishermen. This is actually not the restaurant's name--it has no sign--but it is well known. It is located across from the old Turkish-Egyptian market with the beautiful wooden roof. Don't be put off by its simple appearance; the fish is absolutely fresh that day and is cleaned and barbecued when you order it. The owner says people come from all over Massawa to eat fresh fish and he has his reputation to protect. You receive a plate with freshly barbecued fish (with some lemon if you ask). You eat with your hands and it is customary to finish the meal by squeezing the last of the lemon on the hands and then washing them (there is a special sink for this

inside the restaurant). If you want to eat outside they will put a table in the street for you---there is virtually no traffic in Old Massawa. The restaurant serves mineral water, beer and soft drinks. The fish is delicious: ask for "barracuda" but everything they have is good. A typical meal for four with soft drinks is about 50 birr.

Although shell fish, especially lobsters, are found in Eritrean waters, they are rarely eaten: most people regard their appearance as repulsive.

There are many small restaurants in Massawa serving freshly cooked eggs, salads, fresh bread, faule (the Sudanese bean dish--they will ask you if you want it mixed with a bit of oil or butter) and other snacks.

VISITING THE DHALAK ISLANDS

The Dhalak Islands offer some of the most spectacular scuba diving in the world: crystal-clear water, an abundance of marine life, few visitors, simple but comfortable accomodations, reasonable prices, knowledgeable guides.

Permits are required for travel to the Dahlak Islands, one of Eritrea's most unique areas. The present cost is US $30 per person for up to three days and $10 per person per day thereafter. Check with the Eritrean Tourism Office for the availability of boats. They will also issue the necessary permits.

Scuba Diving

Since the availability of local rental equipment is limited, it is advised that divers bring their own air tanks. Tanks can be provided if arrangements are made well in advance of arrival. Contact Tsegi Berhan at the Tourism Office, tel: 55 28 39.

Scuba divers must be accompanied by a Ministry of Marine Resources (MMR) diver-guide to ensure adherence to the relevant rules and regulations regarding environmental damage to the fragile reefs and marine life.

An MMR diver is required for each six visiting divers who are required to pay for his room and board.

The number of diver-guides is limited and it is essential to make these arrangments prior to arrival in Massawa.

Sport Fishing

Sport fishing in the Red Sea is allowed with a permit. This costs US $30 for three days. This can be obtained at the Red Sea Hotel or from the local branch of the Eritrean Tourism Office.

Due to years of overfishing, no fishing is allowed in inland waters.

Hunting
Due to the descimation of wildlife during the struggle for independence and the need to allow herds to return to adequate numbers, hunting, for the foreseeable future, has been prohibited.

ORGANIZATION OF THE GOVERNMENT

In May 1991 the Eritrean People's Liberation Front defeated Ethiopian military forces and set up the Provisional Government of Eritrea (PGE). In May 1992 the PGE established a governmental structure to administer the country until a United Nations supervised referendum could be held in March 1993. More than 99.8% of the electorate voted for independence from Ethiopia during the referendum. After the referendum, the Government of the State of Eritrea was established with a four year mandate to govern the country. A Constitutional Commission is preparing the new constitution and elections for a permanent government will be held prior to May, 1997. The current government consists of executive (president), legislative and judicial branches, with the following departments, commissions, authorities and offices.

The Eritrean People's Liberation Front (EPLF) which led the country to Independence has reorganized itself into the People's Front for Democracy and Justice (PFDJ).

At present virtually the entire Government administration is based in Asmara. However there is a policy of decentralization and in the near future some ministries will move to nearby towns or to Massawa.

REA

GOVERNMENT OFFICES, ADDRESSES AND TELEPHONE NUMBERS

MINISTRIES OF:	Address/ P.O. Box	Telephone	Fax
Agriculture	1024	18-1499	18-1415
Construction	841	11-9077	none
Defense	629	11-5493	12-61-93
Education	5610	11-3044	11-3866
Energy, Mining and Water Resources	5285	11-6872 12-7944	12-7652
Finance and Development	893	11-3633	11-7947
Foreign Affairs	190	11-3811 11-7700	12-3788
Health	212	11-2877	11-2899
Information and Culture	24	11-5171	12-4847
Internal Affairs	250	11-9299	12-6193
Justice	241	11-1822	none
Local Government	225	11-2055	none
Marine Resources	923	12-4271	11-2185
Tourism	1010	12-3941 12-6997	12-6949
Trade and Industry	1844	11-7806	11-0586
Transport	204	11-0144 11-2241	12-7048
AUTHORITIES OF:			
Communications and	234	11-2900	11-2904
Postal Authority	229	11-5343	11-0938
Port and Maritime Transport Authority	851	12-1399	12- 3647
Social Affairs Authority	5252	11-3763 11-9993	none
Civil Aviation Authority	252	18-2769	18-1255
COMMISSIONS OF:			
Commission for Eritrean Refugee Affairs (CERA)	198	11-2495	12-3502
Housing Commission	348	12-7400	none
Land Commission	976	11-6977 11-2942	12-5123
Sport Division	1500	11-0500	none

GOVERNMENT OFFICES, ADDRESSES AND TELEPHONE NUMBERS

OTHER GOVERNMENT AGENCIES:

	Address/ P.O. Box	Telephone	Fax
Attorney General	249	11-1723	none
Asmara Administration	259	12-4333 12-4599	none
Auditor General	912	12-3523	none
Bank of Eritreal (Governor)	849	12-3033 11-4895	11-3162
Central Personnel Agency	256	11-8884 11-4815	
Chamber of Commerce	859	12-1388 12-1589	12-0138
Commercial Bank of Eritrea	219	12-1844	12-4887
Eritrean Relief and Rehabilitation Agency (ERRA)	1098	11-8300 11-8235	11-2861
Eritrean Television	872	11-1855	12-4847
Eritrean Tour Service 61 Harnet Avenue, Asmara		12-4929	none
High Court (Supreme Court)	241	11-9799	11-2193
Investment Center	921	11-8822 11-9293	12-4293
Labor Office	185	12-2329 11-0977	12-0518
National Insurance Corporation of Eritrea	881	12-3000 12-2256	12-3240
Newspaper "Hadas Eritrea"	247	11-6266 11-7090	none
Office of the President	257	11-9701	12-5123
Radio "Demtsi Hafash"	242	11-9933	12-4847
State Council	257	11-9701	12-5123
University of Asmara	1220	11-0809	11-3831

CRITREAN CMBASSICS ABROAD

Australia, 26 Guilfoyle St., Yarralumia, ACT Canberra, 2600,
Tel: 6-2823489, Fax: 6-2825233.

Belgium, 382 Avenue Louise, B1050 Brussels, Tel: 32-2-6442401,
Fax: 32-2-6442399

China, Peoples Republic, Ta Yuan Ran Gong Lou, 1-4-2, No. 4 South
Liang Maho Rd, Chao Yang District, Beijing PRC, Tel: 1-5326534,
1-5326535, Fax: 1-5326532.

Djibouti, P.O. Box 1944, Djibouti, Tel: 355187,354961, Fax: 351831.

Egypt, P.O. Box 2624, 87 Shahab St., Al Muhandesein, Cairo,
Tel: 3030516, Fax: 3030517.

Ethiopia, P. O. Box 2175, Addis Ababa, Tel: 514302, 512692, Fax: 514911.

Germany, Markstrasse 8, 50968, Koln, Tel: 221-373016 Fax: 221-3404128

Italy, Via Boncompagni 16, Int. 6, 00187 Roma, Tel: 4741293, Fax: 486806

Kenya, P.O. Box 38651, New Woumin House, 4th Floor, West Ianols,
Nairobi, Tel: 443164, Fax: 443165.

Saudi Arabia, Ahmed Lary St., P.O. Box 770, Juddah, Tel: 6612263,
Fax: 6612014.

Sudan, P.O. Box 8129, Khartoum, Tel: 451019, 451037, Fax: 452256

Sweden, Ostermalmsgatan 34, Box 26068, 10041 Stockholm,
Tel: 08- 201470, Fax: 08-206606

United Arab Emirates, P.O. Box 2597, Abu Dhabi, Tel: 2-331838, 2-326255,
Fax: 2-346451

United States of America, 910 17th Street NW, Sute 400, Washington,
D.C. 20006, Tel: 202-429-1991, Fax: 202-429-9004.

Yemen, P.O. Box 11040, Sanaa, Tel: 209422, Fax: 009671, 214088

CONSULATES OF ERITREA

United Kingdom, 96 White Lion Street, London N19PF, Tel: 071-713- 0096, Fax: 071-713-0161.

Canada, 75 Albert Street, #610, Ottawa, Ontario Canada KIP 5E7 Tel. 613-234-3989 Fax: 613-234-6213

UNITED NATIONS

Permanent Mission of Eritrea to the UN, 211 East 43rd St. Suite 2203, New York, N.Y., 10017, Tel: 212-687-3390, Fax: 212-687-3138.

Contact Address:
Switzerland, UNTES, C.P. (P.O. Box) 137, 1211 Geneve 8 Jonction, Tel: 3204913, Fax 3204567.

BILATERAL AGENCIES IN ASMARA

Alliance Francaise
P.O. Box 209, Asmara
Tel: 113499, Fax: 126599

British Council
P.O. Box 5565, Asmara
Tel: 113415, Fax: 121685

GTZ Germany
P.O. Box 5551
Tel: 126581, Fax: 121685

Italian Cooperation
P.O. Box 220
Tel: 120445, 124563, Fax: 113017

United States Agency for International Development
P.O. Box 957
Tel: 123205, 121895, Fax: 871-1514-520

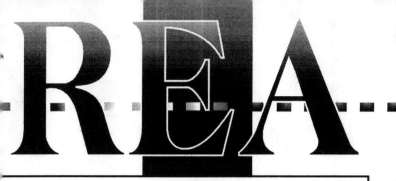

INTERNATIONAL NON-GOVERNMENTAL ORGANIZATIONS (NGOS)

Accord UK
P.O. Box 5538, Asmara
Tel: 118921

Catholic Relief Services
P.O. Box 5617, Asmara
Tel: 120509, Fax: 120791

Christian Outreach
P.O. Box 5617, Asmara
Tel: 120791, Fax: 120791

FKP (GTZ Germany)
P.O. Box 254, Asmara
Tel: 117008, Fax: 120314

International Federation of Red Cross and Red Crescent
P.O. Box 575, Asmara
Tel: 120929, Fax: 122529

Lutheran World Relief, World Service-Eritrea
P.O. Box 773, Asmara
Tel: 122529, Fax: 122529

Norwegian Church Aid
P.O. Box 860, Asmara
Tel: 127718, 121761, Fax: 121221

OXFAM, UK
P.O. Box 5237, Asmara
Tel: 181821, Fax: 181821

Radda Barnen
P.O. Box 5402, Asmara
Tel: 123785, Fax: 123785

Redd Barna
P.O. Box 5232, Asmara
Tel: 124466, Fax: 124466

Save the Children Fund, UK
P.O. Box 555, Asmara
Tel: 122417, Fax: 122417

Voluntary Service Overseas
P.O. Box 5565, Asmara
Tel: 117386, Fax: 116620

World Vision International
P.O. Box 2328, 4 Kidane Mariam Street, Asmara
Tel: 127184

LOCAL NON-GOVERNMENTAL ORGANIZATIONS

National Union of Eritrean Women
P.O. Box 239, Asmara
Tel: 115172, 119514, Fax: 120628

National Confederation of Eritrean Workers
P.O. Box 1188, Asmara
Tel: 116187, Fax: 126606

National Confederation of Eritrean Youth & Students
P.O. Box 1045, Asmara
Tel: 110099, 114386, Fax: 125981

Planned Parenthood Association
P.O. Box 226, Asmara
Tel: 127333, Fax: 120194

Red Cross Society of Eritrea
P.O. Box 575, Asmara
Tel: 120922, 127857, Fax: 124198

MULTILATERAL AGENCIES

European Union
P.O. Box 1117, Asmara
Tel: 122717, Fax: 122717

International Office of Migration
P.O. Box 202, Asmara
Tel: 181615

UNITED NATIONS

Desert Locust Control Organization for Eastern Africa
P.O. Box 231, Asmara
Tel: 113595, 112624

UN Department of Humanitarian Affairs (DHA)
P.O. Box 5366, Asmara
Tel: 182168, 182533, Fax: 873-150-7653

UN High Commission for Refugees (UNHCR)
P.O. Box 1995, Asamara
Tel: 124022, Fax: 873-175-4313

UN International Children's Educational Fund (UNICEF)
P.O. Box 2004, Asmara
Tel: 182533, 181344, Fax: 873-161-0741)

UN World Food Programme (WFP)
P.O. Box 1229, Asmara
Tel: 126669, 120371, Fax: 873-11-51-162

UN World Health Organization (WHO)
P.O. Box 5561, Asmara
Tel: 121901, Fax: 121901

United Nations Development Programme (UNDP)
P.O. Box 5366, Asmara
Tel: 182166, 182533, Fax: 873-150-7653

FOREIGN REPRESENTATIONS-EMBASSIES AND CONSULATES IN ERITREA

Consulate of the United Kingdom
P.O. Box 5584, Asmara, Tel: 120145 Fax: 120104

Embassy of the People's Republic of China
P.O. Box 204, Asmara, #6 Arbagugu Street, Tel: 11-6988   Fax: 157-2123 (satellite)

Embassy of the Republic of Djibouti,
P.O. Box 5589, Asmara, Tel: 182189, Fax: 181001.

Embassy of the Arab Republic of Egypt
P.O. Box 5570, Asmara, Tel: 123603, 124935, Fax: 121115

Embassy of the Transitional Government of Ethiopia
Franklin D. Roosevelt Street, Tel: 116144, 111500

Embassy of the State of Israel
P.O. Box 5600, Asmara, Tel: 120137, Fax: 120187

Embassy of the Italian Republic
P.O. Box 220, Asmara, Tel: 120160, 120774, Fax: 121115.

Embassy of the United States of America
P.O. Box 211, Asmara, Tel: 123720, 123410, Fax: 127584.

Embassy of the Republic of Yemen
P.O. Box 5566, Asmara, Tel: 120208, 118962, Fax: 118962.

Representative of the Norwegian Authorities
P.O. Box 860, Asmara, Tel: 127718, 121761, Fax: 121221

ERIT

MAPS

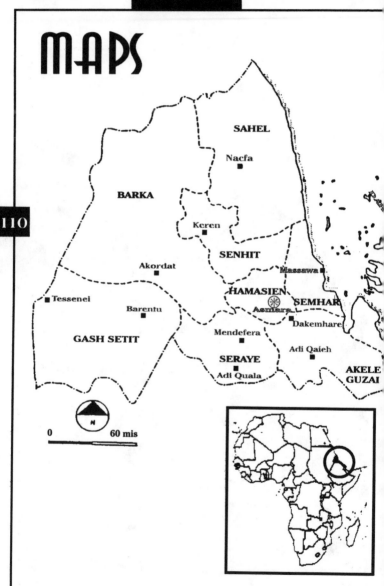

TREA...

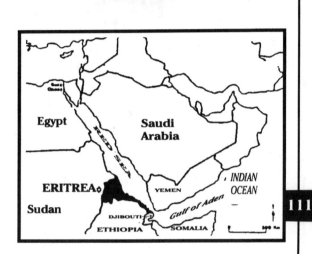

Eritrea with provinces and their capitals

DENKALIA

Assab

ERIT

INDEX

Abeba Tesfagiorgis, 35
Abyssinian kingdom, 15
Accord UK, 105
Addis Ababa, 17, 28, 29,
    31, 103
Adi Qayeh, 13
Adi Quala, 85, 86
Adulis, 15, 90
Afar, 37, 96
Afar Fish Restaurant, 96
Afars, 13
Africa World Press, 35
Agricultural resources, 10
Akele Guzai, 13
Akordat, 13, 38
Alliance Francaise, 59, 104
Ambasoira Hotel, 11, 57, 62, 63
Ambassador Hotel, 11, 64, 70
Ambulance, 60
Arabic, 8, 26, 37, 59, 60
Arab Republic of Egypt, 108
Arbaete Asmara, 52
Archaeology Museum, 74
Ark of the Covenant, 86
Asmara, 8, 10-13, 17, 19, 22-25,
    28-30, 34, 35, 38-42, 46, 48, 50,
    52, 54-60, 62-71, 74-76, 92,
    94, 96, 100, 102,
    104-108
Asmara football stadium, 83
Asmara Restaurant, 68
Asmara Theatrical Society, 83
Assab, 10, 11, 13, 25, 31, 42, 89
Australia, 103
Awget Bookstore, 60
Axum, 15, 86, 90
Axumite kingdom, 15, 90

Bar Trestelle, 80
Bar Vittoria, 59, 70, 80, 81
Baraka harbor, 32, 93
Barentu, 13
Barka, 13
Beilul, 90
Beilul Restaurant, 68
Beja kingdoms, 15
Belgium, 103
Bereket Habte Selassie, 35
Bilen, 13, 37
Bologna Restaurant, 69
British Council, 59, 104
British Council Library, 59

Cafe Impero, 80
Cairo, 30, 103
Camping, 65, 95
Campo Estato, 52
Canada, 23, 104
Caravel Restaurant and Hotel, 69
Castello Restaurant, 69
Cathedral Snack Bar, 80, 81
Catholic Cathedral, 54, 77, 80
Catholic Relief Services, 105
Central Hospital,
    Makane Hiwot, 60
Central Post Office, 56
Chamber of Commerce, 102
China, Peoples Republic, 103, 108
Christian Outreach, 105
Christmas, 44
Cinema Dante, 65
Cinemas, 78
City Park, 80
City Park Cafe, 80

112

INDEX

City Hall, 76
CNN, 63
Commercial Bank, 102
Connell, Dan, 35
Constitutional Commission, 100
Consulate of United
       Kingdom, 108
Consulates of Eritrea, 104
Currency, 25

Danakil desert, 13
Dankalia, 13, 42
Dankalia Depression, 42
Daro Kunaat, 86
Debre Bizen Monastery, 92
Dekemhare, 57
Denden, 17, 78
Dergue, the, 18, 19, 62, 78, 86,
       90, 94
Dhalak Hotel, 11, 94
Dhalak Islands, 93, 98
DHL, 57
Djibouti, 8, 13, 103, 108

Egypt, 11, 15, 16, 28, 103, 108
Egypt Air, 11, 28
Eid al-Adha, 44
Eid al-Fitr, 44
Eid al-Nabi, 44
Elaberiet, 84
Embassy of
       Italian Republic, 108
       Republic of Yemen, 108
       Arab Republic of Egypt, 108
       People's Republic of
              China, 108

Republic of Djibouti, 108
State of Israel, 108
Transitional Government of
       Ethiopia, 108
United States of America, 108
Emergencies, 60
Enda Mariam (St. Mary's) Orthodox
       Christian Church, 76
English, 8, 17, 26, 35, 45, 58-60,
       66, 68, 70, 96
Eritrean Airlines, 11, 28, 72
Eritrean diplomatic
       representations, 103
Eritrean Liberation Front, 18
Eritrean Medical Association, 35
Eritrean People's
       Liberation Front (EPLF), 18, 19,
       50, 100
Eritrean Relief and Rehabilitation
       Agency, 35, 102
Eritrean Television, 102
Eritrean Tour Service, 41, 42,
       56, 86, 93, 94, 102
Eritrea Profile, 35, 60, 66
Eritrea Restaurant, 96
Ethiopia, 8, 13, 15-19, 29, 31, 58, 74,
       75, 78, 81, 86, 87, 90, 100,
       103, 108
Ethiopian Airlines, 11, 28, 29, 31
Ethnographic Museum, 74, 75
European Union, 106
Expo Hotel and Sauna, 64, 69
Expo Restaurant, 69

Fascists, 16, 86
Fasika, 44
Fax Services, 57, 62

INDEX

Federal Express, 58
Federation, 17
Fire Department, 60
FKP (GTZ Germany), 105
Foreign representations-
    embassy's and
    consulates in Eritrea, 108
Franciscan Cathedral, 77
Frankfurt, 30
Funj sultanates, 15

114

Gash & Setit, 13
Ge'ez calender, 22
Gedaref, 30
Germany, 103, 104, 105
Ghinda, 85, 92
Government Agencies, 102
Government of Eritrea, 10, 23,
    100
Government offices, 101
Great Britain, 16, 23
GTZ Germany, 104
Gurgusum Beach Hotel, 95
Gurgusum Beach, 11, 95

Haddas Eritrea, 60
Haile Selassie, 16-18, 22, 74
Hamasien, 13
Hamasien Hotel, 11, 63, 95
Hedareb, 13, 37
Hunting, 99

Impero, 78
Independence Day, 13, 20, 44
Institute of Research and
    Development, 59

International Federation of
    Red Cross and
    Red Crescent, 105
International NGOs, 105
International Office of
    Migration, 107
International telephone
    operator, 57
International Vaccination Card, 23
Islam, 15
Islamic Learning Centre, 59
Israel, 108
Italian colonialism, 10, 15,
    31, 54, 56
Italian Cooperation, 104
Italian Hospital, 60
Italian, 26, 58
Italian Republic, 108
Italy, 15, 16, 70, 86, 87, 103

Jamie al-Khulafa'e
    al-Rashidin Mosque, 76
Jeddah, 30

Kagnew Base, 17, 78
Kassala, 30
Kenya, 34, 55, 90, 103
Keren, 11, 13, 38, 84
Keren Hotel, 11, 60, 64, 68, 84
Keren Hotel Restaurant, 67, 68
Khartoum, 30, 103
Keneally, Thomas, 35
Kunama, 13, 37

Legesse Hotel, 65, 70
Legesse Hotel Restaurant, 70

REA

INDEX

Lidet, 44
Local NGOs, 106
local telephone information, 57
Lufthansa, 11, 30
Lutheran World Relief, World
        Service-Eritrea, 105

Martyr's Day, 44
Massawa, 10-13, 15, 19, 25,
        31, 38, 42, 56-58, 65, 85,
        86, 89-98, 100
Medeber, 75
Mendefera, 13, 57, 58, 85, 86
Mengistu Haile Mariam, 18, 19
Meskel, 44
Military Museum, 75
Mineral reserves, 10
Mineral water, 67-69, 96, 97
Ministry of Agriculture, 58, 85,
        101
Ministry of Marine Resources
        and Fisheries, 58, 98, 101
Ministry of Tourism, 42, 94, 101
Municipal Library, 59
Murara, 84, 85
Mussolini, 16, 31

Nacfa, 13
Nafasit, 38, 92
Nara, 13, 37
National Confedration of
        Eritrean Workers, 106
National Museum, 48, 58, 74, 80
National Union of Eritrean
        Women, 35, 106
National Confederation
        of Eritrean Youth
        and Students, 106

Neguse G, 81
New Massawa, 93, 94
Norwegian Church Aid, 105
Norwegian Authorities,
        Representative of, 108
Nyala Hotel, 11, 58, 64, 68-70

Odeon, 78
Old Massawa, 32, 91, 93, 94,
        96, 97
Opera House, 78
Organization of African
        Unity (OAU), 17, 18
Orota, 19, 75
Orthodox Cathedral, 75
Orthodox Church, 54
Orthodx Christianity, 8, 15, 86
Ottoman Turks, 15
Our Lady of the Rosary
        Cathedral, 77
OXFAM, UK, 105

Papstein, Robert , 35
Pateman, Roy, 35
People's Front for Democracy
        and Justice, 100
People's Republic of China, 108
Pizzaria Napoli, 70
Planned Parenthood
        Association, 106
Police, 11, 17, 60
Provisional Government
        of Eritrea, 10, 19, 59, 100

Radda Barnen, 105
Radio Demtsi Hafash, 102

115

INDEX

Rashaida, 13, 37
Re'esee Ketema, 70
Red Cross Society of Eritrea, 106
Red Sea, the, 8, 10, 13, 15, 19, 68, 89-93, 98
Red Sea Grocery, 96
Red Sea Hotel, 11, 93, 94, 98
Red Sea Press, 12, 35
Redd Barna, 105
Referendum, 10, 19, 20, 56, 100
Republic of Djibouti, 108
Republic of Yemen, 108
Roma, 78
Roman Catholicism, 8, 77
Royal Cafe, 80

Sahel, 13, 18, 19
Saho, 13, 37
Saint Mary of Zion monastry complex, 86
Sanaa, 30, 103
Saudia Airlines, 11, 30
Saudi Arabia, 8, 15, 16, 93, 103
Save the Children Fund, UK, 106
Scuba diving, 98
Selam Hotel, 11
Selam Hotel, 11, 63
Semhar, 13
Semienawi Bahri, 79
Senai Grocery, 72
Senhit, 13, 84
Sennar, 15
Seraye, 13, 85
Serejeka, 84, 85
Shuk, 75
Sobur, 84, 85

Somalia, 16, 90
Soviet Union, 18, 19
Sport fishing, 98
St. George Restaurant, 68
State of Israel, 108
Suakin, 90
Sudan, 8, 13, 15, 16, 30, 45, 81, 90, 103
Sudan Airways, 11, 30
Sudanese restaurants, 71
Sweden, 103
Switzerland, 104

Tank graveyard, 78
Telephone, 11, 22, 57, 58, 60, 62-65, 94, 101, 102
    international operator, 11
    local information, 11
The Struggle, 14, 1822, 35, 47, 50, 75, 79, 99
Tigrai People's Liberation Front (TPLF), 86
Tigre, 13, 37
Tigrinya, 8, 13, 26, 37, 52, 59, 60, 63, 68, 70, 80
Timket, 44, 86
TNT International, 58
Tourist information, 23
Transitional Government of Ethiopia, 108
Tsetserat, 78

UN Department of Humanitarian Affairs (DHA), 107

INDEX

UN High Commission for
Refugees (UNHCR), 107
UN International Children's
Educational Fund (UNICEF), 107
UN Wold Health Organization
(WHO), 107
UN World Food Programme
(WFP), 107
United Arab Emirates, 103
United Kingdom, 23, 104, 108
United Nations Development
Program (UNDP), 107
United Nations, 1619, 100, 104, 107
United States, 17, 23, 42, 59,
103, 104, 108
University of Asmara, 58, 102
USA, 10, 12, 23, 25, 31, 39, 45, 46
USAID, 104

Visas , 28
Voluntary Service Overseas, 106

Weki, 84
Women's Day, 44
World Vision International, 106

Yemen, 8, 93, 103, 108
Yemenia Airlines, 11, 30

Zager, 84
Zegereda/Rose Hotel, 65

117

ASMARA CENTER CITY MAP 1:7000

...ERIT...

NOTES

P 41 — Cape hire details

REA...

NOTES

NOTES

REA

NOTES

NOTES

REA

NOTES

NOTES

REA

NOTES

ERITREA

NOTES